Reinventing Scale-Ups

Reinventing Scale-Ups

Radical Ideas for Growing Companies

Second Edition

Brent Lowe

Susan Basterfield

Travis Marsh

Edited by Nicole Petrak

We owe a sincere debt of gratitude to all of those who have helped with this book.

Alanna Irving
Anthony Cabraal
Bob Vaez
Brian Spears
Bryan Peters
Bryan Ungard
Catherine Mulvale
Daniel Rose
David Horowitz
Doug Kirkpatrick
Edwin Jansen
Francesca Pick
Frederic Laloux
Gina Rembe
Greg Judelman
Heiko Fischer
Helen Sanderson
Joshua Vial
Kate Beecroft
Kate Fulton
Kazimeirz Gozdz
Keith McCandless
Kim Davidson
Kim Scott
Kurtis McBride
Luz Iglesias
Michael Göthe
Mike McDerment
Natalie Dumond
Ray Cao
Ria Baeck
Richard Sheridan
Rosie Lawn
Samantha Slade
Sean O'Connor
Ved Krishna
Victor Vorski
Our families for your enduring support

And the Teal for Startups Community.
Without you, we would have
never connected in the first place.

CONTENTS

INTRODUCTION

Kurtis McBride scanned the leadership section of his local bookstore. As a new CEO, he needed help. His company, Miovision, was making headway. He and his co-founders had discovered a market pain point they could solve, and as a result, the three-person startup had grown to 60 employees. Kurtis needed to turn this collection of talented people into a thriving, scalable company.

This excursion to the bookstore was one of many. An engineer by training, Kurtis believed research and reading was critical to growing a successful business. He made his selection and headed home to start learning tried and proven strategies for structuring an organization.

Armed with these "best practices," and needing to manage an expanding workload, Kurtis started shaping Miovision as a traditional hierarchy. It was a logical next step…

It didn't work.

Instead of helping him scale up, Miovision became mired in bureaucracy. The entrepreneurial energy and spirit critical to the company's initial growth began to erode. So Kurtis went back to the bookstore and bought more books. Iterating different approaches over several years, Kurtis and his team created their own unique way of structuring the organization. Miovision has since scaled to over 160 employees with revenues increasing by a factor of ten.

*Reinventing Scale-Up*s is the book Kurtis couldn't find on his trips to the bookstore. It turns out he didn't need a step-by-step best practices guide. Miovision needed its own unique solution and Kurtis needed fresh ideas.

We empathize with the challenges faced by courageous entrepreneurs like Kurtis. Great risk and adventure accompanies building an organization that attracts talented people, builds products or delivers services to solve important problems, and doesn't believe purposeful work and financial benefits are mutually exclusive.

We wrote *Reinventing Scale-Ups* for founders who work passionately to positively impact the world. We profile unique and radical ways scale-ups—organizations outgrowing their startup roots—have adapted to meet their specific needs. You will find practical, tactical tips to stimulate your thinking and help you shape your organization.

All the companies in *Reinventing Scale-Ups* began as startups. Some are still in the early stages of finding their way, while others have grown significantly. We share their learnings here to inspire you in creating your own ideal solutions.

So What Is A Scale-up?

Is a scale-up measured by team size? Revenue? Number of customers? Speed of growth? Any or all the above? We'll leave that debate for another time. Our aim is to speak to the challenges faced by founders of growing businesses. We've focused on companies that have made it through their first couple of years, are sustainable in their current configuration and are actively considering "What's next for our organization?"

Leaders of scale-ups face a whole new set of challenges and a steep learning curve. The requirements and opportunities for personal and professional growth that span decades in other roles and organization types are concentrated into a few short years.

Before heading into the practical chapters which follow, it's useful to understand our foundational beliefs and how they shaped the content. Why have we chosen to focus on some companies and not others? Where do we believe the future is headed? A few different schools of thought have influenced our writing. We are inspired by the work of Frederic Laloux (*Reinventing Organizations*),[1] Robert Kegan (*An Everyone Culture: Becoming a Deliberately Developmental Organization*),[2] and Dr. Brené Brown (*The Gifts of Imperfection*[3]; "The Power of Vulnerability").[4] In addition to reading, we have spent the last two years traveling the world, both physically and virtually, to learn from the best forward thinkers in this space.

An organization cannot evolve beyond its leadership's stage of development.

– Frederic Laloux

Through our work we have come to embrace five principles which have been woven into the chapters that follow. We believe these are essential to building an impactful and thriving organization. These principles are anchored in the belief that investing in creating the right environment increases the probability of scaling up a sustainable, prosperous company.

Principle #1: Meaningful work is enhanced through purpose beyond profit. When we unearth a clear, shared and inspiring purpose beyond the profit motive, work becomes more meaningful and fulfilling for everyone.

Principle #2: Organizations evolve and require freedom to emerge over time. The character and capabilities of an organization surface as its participants experiment with possibilities until a workable system appears.

Principle #3: (Psychological) Safety leads to creativity and learning. When we invite our colleagues to bring their full selves to work, free of fear and personal judgement, creativity and learning follow.

Principle #4: Business challenges provide a natural learning curriculum. Deliberately leveraging the needs of the business as a platform for personal development allows for ongoing business growth. Business growth, in turn, creates new opportunities for personal development.

Principle #5: Transparency and having a say enhances accountability. When everyone in an organization has access to the same information, is invited to provide opinions, and is entrusted to make decisions, the result is shared context, ownership and a sense of accountability.

Now is a good time to ask yourself, "Do I want to lead a business that follows a well-worn path or do I believe my company should be different?"

We like to question long-held beliefs about what makes a truly successful business. Although most of the ideas that follow are not yet widely embraced, they have been tested and honed with a variety of early stage companies introduced throughout the book.

We believe the world needs you to be successful. With over 50 collective years working with startups and scale-ups across five continents, we are passionate about supporting founders. It is your work that will lead us all into the future.

We do not profess to have all the answers for your unique circumstances. Instead, we believe you are best-positioned to be your own case study—learning, iterating and growing. Our goal is to provoke new thoughts and invite experimentation. **As you experiment, we invite you to share your stories and connect with us on Facebook at https://www.facebook.com/groups/ ReinventingScaleUps.**

Warning: By pursuing the ideas that follow, you will be seen as an outlier and a rebel.

Chapter 1

WHY THIS BOOK? WHY NOW?

THE DRIVERS OF CHANGE

In 2001, the Agile Manifesto was released.[1] It defined a new way for software teams to work; a new set of values:

Individuals and interactions over processes and tools
Working software over comprehensive documentation
Customer collaboration over contract negotiation
Responding to change over following a plan

Since then, agile methodologies have transformed software creation. They have changed how people work together and organize themselves. Agile teams engage in events that keep everyone focused on the most important work. Team members are accountable for the work they do and are expected to share their individual strengths with the team.

These teams communicate transparently. They self-organize, aligning around the work that needs to be done. They support one another and hold each other accountable. They look for continuous improvement opportunities and adapt quickly. They value coaching as an indispensable way to help people develop. They are **self-managing**.

Frederic Laloux published *Reinventing Organizations* in 2014. His game-changing curation of organizations working not as machines, but as living systems, opened a window into companies that embrace a different model for business. Morning Star, FAVI, W. L. Gore and Buurtzorg may not be household names but their teams are pioneers in new ways of working. The leaders of the companies Frederic profiled foster environments of trust, autonomy and openness where hierarchies are replaced by fluid ecosystems. Frederic's book shows how the self-management values inherent in agile software development now permeate entire organizations in many different types of businesses.

Self-management can be conceptualized as a scaffolding rather than as a framework. Frameworks are brittle by nature. Once you start adding bricks, mortar and drywall onto a frame, change is difficult. Scaffolding allows you to reorient to suit your unique situation at any moment in time.

Agile software products offer another helpful analogy. Software is emergent. Despite advance planning and clear intention, you are rarely sure of what, exactly, you are building until the product is complete. It only emerges through many iterations. The same can be said for how organizations incubate, grow and evolve. There are no step-by-step guides for self-management. There are only ideas, experiments and iterations as you shape your own scaffolding.

In *Reinventing Scale-Ups*, we will show how the shift to a more agile, ecosystem-like approach is unfolding within companies. But first, let's talk about why the dogma of the past is unravelling. Why are companies compelled to experiment and look for new ways of working?

Three tensions are increasing with time. These tensions are leading scale-ups to struggle with traditional pyramid structures and associated management principles. Each tension is experienced by team members of scale-ups, but not always by the founders of the business who are less constrained by the organizational structure.

Tension #1: How we make decisions in our organization is slow and frustrating.

With technology transforming industries, the need for quick decision-making is increasing; yet the supporting tools and approaches used in the workplace remain relatively unchanged. Before email, Slack and YouTube, a pyramid structure helped move knowledge efficiently through an organization. Information flowed from the bottom to the top of the pyramid where a manager or leader compiled, processed, and made decisions based on the data available. Those decisions were then sent back down the pyramid to be acted upon. This approach worked reasonably well at slower speeds.

With the need to move faster, eliminating bottlenecks is a top priority, and finding ways to share decision-making throughout the organization becomes a necessity. Without updated decision-making tools, team members find themselves caught between their need to quickly make good decisions, and business frameworks which slow them down.

Tension #2: I don't have access to the RIGHT information to make good decisions.

"With the internet, I can easily get information on pretty much anything, but at work I can't access the information I need." We are becoming conditioned to expect easy access to real time information in all parts of our lives.

For many, this is in direct contrast to conditions at work. Whether due to a shortage of systems, poor organization or lack of transparency, scale-ups that don't prioritize free-flowing information suffer from an inability to make good, informed decisions quickly. More than ever, your colleagues have an expectation that data will be readily-accessible.

Tension #3: Good ideas seem unnecessarily correlated with tenure.

In our relatively new online world, the best ideas get up-voted and rise to the top. A university student has the same ability to have a winning idea as a seasoned business leader. There is a heightened expectation and understanding that good ideas can come from anyone, anywhere. Who leads and who follows emerges naturally and may shift over time.

Traditional business frameworks, in contrast, are rigid and unchanging. Leadership is based on title and authority. Ideas usually come from the top and roles are assigned. Team members find themselves frustrated and demotivated by artificial constraints misaligned with the organic nature of other parts of their lives.

The good news is that fresh approaches are emerging to help businesses adjust to a new, more agile world and overcome these tensions. Dogma is unhelpful, especially when rooted in yesterday's reality. Life is constantly changing. Embrace the change. The following chapters invite you to carve your own unique path for your company.

A quick word on why this book is stamped with Beta 2.0 on the cover. As authors, we fully embrace agile and self-management methodologies. Technology allows us to print *Reinventing Scale-Ups* on-demand and make updates easily. Based on feedback from readers of Beta 1.0, we have changed the book title, added and re-written chapters, and expanded on ideas. We hope you find this version helpful.

The World Has Changed.

"I played my first video game when I was nine. It was Pong. There were five friends in the neighborhood to play Pong with. Life was simple.

My friend's daughter Carmel is nine. She has 225,000 followers on musical.ly. Last month she received an endorsement contract.

I started my first business when I was seventeen. At the time, state-of-the-art technology included a fax machine and pager.

Carmel's brother is fourteen. He's running his first online business. He's part of a startup accelerator program.

Our world has evolved. How we work must evolve too."

– Brent

Chapter 2

LOOKING INWARD FIRST

AUTHORITY, BELIEFS ABOUT PEOPLE AND LEADERSHIP

A common belief about leadership assumes that a well-performing business is a reflection of the collective strengths and contributions of the team, and conversely, that every dysfunction can be traced back to poor leadership. True or not, it's hard to downplay the impact founders have in creating flourishing teams. For this reason, and before we can dig into radical ideas for shaping the organization, we first need to look inward.

Leadership and *power* are possibly the two most loaded words in business. This is especially true for organizations trying to be different. Traditional businesses operate using command-and-control, top-down management. Emerging business philosophies prioritize responsibility and freedom. In theory, it's easy to see how supporting individual responsibility is preferable to a do-what-I-say approach. In practice, it's much harder to implement.

SideFX is a 30-year-old, 80-person visual effects software company and a global leader in their space. Despite its age, the company still has the feel of an early-stage, scaling business. Kim Davidson is a co-founder and has held the position of CEO since inception. Immensely passionate about his industry, he is beloved by his team and customers. Kim continues to steward the business through year-over-year growth.

Prior to embarking on a recent refresh of SideFX's vision, purpose and values, Kim was asked for his thoughts on what these elements should be going forward. His answer was immediate and resolute.

"I don't know, ask the team. They are in the best position to decide."

When pushed for a sense of direction, Kim's answer didn't change: "Really, this isn't up to me alone. The team knows what's working and what isn't."

Kim stayed true to his word, allowing the team both the freedom and responsibility of charting the next phase of the company's journey. He remained an active contributor throughout the project but provided little direction, making only minor tweaks. In the end, the team was heavily invested in the changes and he was fully aligned with the result. This is how Kim has led his team since day one. He readily admits that even after 30 years of experience, he continues to learn daily how to lead.

In an ideal world, everyone on your team would show up fully capable, knowing exactly what to do and how to do it. The team would be perfectly coordinated, workloads would be perfectly balanced, and business growth would be perfectly smooth.

You would know exactly what to say and do to steward optimal progress.

Every founder can attest that this is never the case.

How do you want to "show up" as a leader within your company, especially in the chaotic moments?

The SideFX story demonstrates three beliefs we see inherent in the mindsets of founders of successful "reinvented" scale-ups. These leaders demonstrate the same curiosity, creativity and drive for results we see in all capable founders. They also share common beliefs about **authority, people** and **their own role as a leader**. Let's take a look at these three common beliefs in detail.

Authority Versus Power

When we are children, the authority of our caregivers is important. In our earliest years, those older than us patently know more than we do. They use their authority to protect us from harm and help us learn and grow. The same is true in business. Founders have relevant experience and access to more information than most others in the organization. They often hold a broader perspective and invest passionately in thinking about their company.

Authority and power are different. Authority protects. Power controls. Holding authority does not make you a leader, nor should it make you more powerful. On the contrary, it puts you in a position of service. Power, however, leverages title and position to exert personal will and preference. Power trumps the knowledge, skills and abilities of the team—not for the greater good, but for the individual's desires or wishes.

In the case of SideFX, Kim maintained his authority as CEO throughout the process of redefining the company's vision. All participants understood that Kim, in his role as company steward, would be the final approver of the new vision, purpose and values. He did not, however, use his position as CEO and shareholder to control the process or predetermine the outcome. Kim could have easily used the power of his position to craft and dictate a vision for the future based on his in-depth knowledge and years of experience running SideFX.

> "The servant-leader is servant first... Becoming a servant-leader begins with the natural feeling that one wants to serve, to serve first. Then conscious choice brings one to aspire to lead. That person is sharply different from one who is leader first... The difference manifests itself in the care taken by the servant first to make sure that other people's highest priority needs are being served. The best test, and the most difficult to administer, is this: Do those served grow as persons? Do they, while being served, become healthier, wiser, freer, more autonomous, more likely themselves to become servants?"[1]
>
> – Robert Greenleaf
> Greenleaf Center for Servant Leadership

Exerting power over someone else inherently diminishes the other person. Why build an organization full of powerless people? We can choose instead to leverage the collective to impact our shared environment. Sharing power with others brings everyone onto the same plane; even when specific individuals hold authority, everyone can be powerful. This collective sense of ownership is core to agile and self-managed organizations. It brings people together, builds shared understanding, and fuels group commitment.

In a coaching conversation with a particular founder about authority and power, the founder said "Our ultimate goal is to get stuff done. We don't start companies because we want power. If any startup founder exercises power, it is because they feel it is the best way of getting to the next step or it is their natural style."

This raises an important question. As the leader of your business, is it ever appropriate to exert authority in a way that may feel like "power over"? The answer requires a separation between "what" and "how." In the role of founder and CEO you may, at times, be best positioned to make mission-critical decisions in the best interest of the business. Using the authority and responsibility associated with your role as a steward of the business might be both appropriate and necessary.

The feeling of "power over" experienced by a team comes more from **how** a leader exerts authority. Grabbing control and issuing directives out of frustration and impatience leaves teams feeling powerless. Making critical decisions transparently with a mindset of collective learning leads teams to feel valued and equally powerful. In future chapters, we will explore alternatives to power-based approaches often used by scale-up founders.

While Kim at SideFX naturally limits his power-based decision-making, Kurtis at Miovision is more intentional in his approach. He and his senior team place limits on the number of times they can leverage their positions to make decisions falling within the authority of others' roles. Miovision leaders are permitted to make or overrule decisions outside their direct scope of authority only three times each year. This limitation naturally forces leaders to act as coaches and mentors, keeping decisions where they optimally belong: with their teams.

Making space for others to step into their own authority is challenging. How can you tell if others are making decisions that incur unacceptable risk? What if team choices are equally valid but differ from your own? When do interrelated decisions require centralized coordination? In Chapter 7, we dive deeper into decision-making and how to support your team in this area.

If you would like to experiment, here's a way to get started. **For the next five days, commit to drastically reducing the decisions you make by enabling others on your team to take definitive action.** Each time a decision comes your way, ask yourself three questions:

1. Is someone else on the team capable of making this decision?
2. Does the learning offered to my team in making this decision outweigh the risk to the company?
3. Is the decision reversible if things go awry?

If you can answer yes to these three questions, even if it's uncomfortable, step back and let your team decide. At the end of the five days, evaluate what you've learned. How did it feel? What were the results? How did you react when decisions were made that strayed from your preference? What do you want to try next?

If you were challenged in answering yes to one or more of these three questions, why is that? What can be learned if the answer is no?

Beliefs About People

Do you believe people are fundamentally good and inherently aim to do great work? Or do you believe people generally put themselves first, prioritizing personal gain over what's best for the business? How you show up as a leader depends on which of these two beliefs resonates most.

What types of power are you attached to?

"I'm serving a team in Western Australia as their 1200-person organization transitions to self-organizing teams. The existing executive team members have decided what they, themselves, collectively need: a stronger commitment to disperse their power. Or, as one member puts it, 'We need to come together to break up.' They call this their Transitional Reality. We've been thinking together about power, and its many meanings and definitions. The team tries to notice which of these facets of power they are enacting or, put more bluntly, which power card they are playing by asking:

- Am I attempting to influence the outcome?
- Am I advocating for my preferred solution?
- Am I attempting to add context?
- Am I leveraging my authority?
- Am I trying to reinforce my status?
- Am I taking decisions on my own?
- Am I being a responsible leader?

Members of the team are attracted to—and may more readily demonstrate—different forms of power. The key for them is a willingness to acknowledge and recognize these habits, and disperse some of these decisions to others' roles in ways which are transparent and accountable. That does not mean no one will ever use these forms of power. It does mean that the entire organization will be more aware of when and how they are used."

– Susan

Leaders who connect more with the first statement believe their colleagues are motivated by internal factors such as the opportunity to contribute, learn and grow. In his popular book *Drive*, Dan Pink identifies **autonomy**, **mastery** and **purpose** as primary intrinsic motivators.

The alternative philosophy states that people are motivated by external factors such as **rewards** for good work and **punishment** for poor performance. Achievement-oriented bonuses and strict policy enforcement fall into this category.

The external motivator approach to leadership tends to generate compliance. Back when the Ford Motor Company was a young and scaling business pioneering the use of assembly lines, Henry Ford is rumored to have said, "Why is it every time I ask for a pair of hands, they come with a brain attached?" In this example, Ford was seeking compliance to a defined and repeatable system. He needed hands to run machines but little thinking was required or even desired. When consistency and speed in mechanical tasks is the priority, external motivators can be effective.

Nowadays however, more companies rely on knowledge-based work and creativity. In these areas, clear intention and full engagement are more important than compliance. Founders of reinvented scale-ups invest heavily in strengthening their own abilities to tap into their colleagues' internal motivators. Many examples of tapping internal motivators lie in the pages that follow. Here are a few we will explore in more detail later:

- Distributing appropriate autonomy through decision-making processes.
- Creating an organizational culture rooted in learning and growth.
- Communicating a shared purpose everyone on the team finds meaningful.

The Role of Leader(s)

If your role *isn't* to use power to control the team or leverage external motivation to incentivize behavior, then what is your role? The founders of reinvented scale-ups focus on ensuring five important roles are enacted within the organization. Often founders and CEOs fill these roles directly. They may also consider distributing these roles to those with the most passion or skill. Let's look at these roles in more detail.

Strategist and Inspirer – Someone needs to steward and champion the organization's purpose and strategy. As the individual with the broadest view of the company and marketplace, the founder is often best-suited for this responsibility. Founders tend to be passionate, driven individuals. Teams benefit when that energy is shared in the form of inspiration. It's difficult for everyone on the team to stay focused on the big picture while executing day-to-day operations. Keeping the organization's "North Star" at the forefront and sharing progress updates helps the team remain aligned and focused. We dig into this role further in Chapter 3 on Purpose.

Communication Orchestrator – We started this chapter by comparing a top-down bureaucratic approach to one that is more free-flowing and entrepreneurial. For a team to operate with a greater sense of responsibility and freedom, it needs access to the same information available to the leader. The more transparently information flows through an organization, the more empowered a team will be. Chapter 8 explores transparency in more detail.

Culture Steward – Company culture is formed the day two people start working together. It evolves over time, including when someone new joins. Eventually, it solidifies. Many of the following chapters provide insight into how leaders participate in the co-creation of unique company cultures. Chapter 4 on Psychological Safety is of particular importance.

Culture is a living thing, and like all living things it requires a strong immune system to stay healthy. Cultures are compromised by the worst behaviors demonstrated or permitted by the team. The best cultures are co-created and subsequently kept healthy when the team proactively decides how it will work together. This process inoculates against unhealthy behavior. Culture also requires regular reviews—booster shots—to keep it well and strong.

Resource Balancer – When properly resourced, we do our best work. For scale-ups, resources—most often people and money—are in short supply. Helping your team balance available resources and find new resources is an invaluable role. Chapter 7 will help you shape how decisions about limited resources can be made. Chapters 12 and 13 focus on recruiting and onboarding new team members.

Role-Design Coach – When eager, skilled and empowered people are passionate about their work, magic happens. Helping team members find the sweet spot where their passion aligns with their skills while supporting their continual development is a never-ending puzzle that we explore in Chapter 6.

None of the leaders we've met have been exceptional at all five of these roles, nor do they aim to be. Instead, they show up as imperfect role models on a journey of learning. They understand their colleagues will sometimes make poor decisions, just as they will. Their focus is on creating a deliberately developmental organization where passionate people work towards a common purpose, learning and growing along the way. When things go awry, these leaders look inward first.

If you would like an additional resource to help create a "look-inward-first" mindset, check out *Leadership and Self Deception* by The Arbinger Institute. It follows the story of a CEO transitioning from an outward-looking to an inward-looking leadership approach.

Chapter 3

BRINGING MEANING TO WORK

LEADING WITH PURPOSE

For most of us, being able to engage in purpose-driven and meaningful work is the highest ideal we hope for in our professional lives. After all, for most people, simply securing a livelihood—surviving—is the core motivation for and purpose of work. The ability to align our personal values and tap into our own intrinsic motivators is a wonderful privilege.

Having a "North Star" or guiding reason for your organization's existence is powerful, and also difficult to articulate. A thriving consulting industry exists to help unearth an organization's mission, vision and values—but these statements can easily fall flat and fail to drive the intended behavior. To see an exaggerated example of how trite many of these efforts can be, check out Jon Haworth's free online "Mission Statement Generator."[1]

Beyond the Intellectual Pursuit of Purpose

Meaningful purpose emerges from an organization's big "Why," often over years of reflection and exploration, stewarded by individuals with strong personal values and a shared sense of purpose.

In an attempt to capture and communicate this purpose, we rely on the inadequacy of words in the form of statements. As hard as we try, words remain inanimate. They are important and helpful but insufficient.

"Executives, at least in my experience, don't pause in a heated debate to turn to the company's mission statement for guidance, asking, 'What does our purpose require us to do?'"

– Frederic Laloux

Consider the idea that, beyond its founding, your organization brings to life its own purpose, and the job of everyone in the organization is to listen to what 'it' needs to do next. The idea of an organization having its own "say" may feel bizarre, however consider the following example as an analogy.

A river in New Zealand has recently become the first in the world to be recognized as a living entity with its own rights and values and given the legal status of a person.[2]

The Whanganui River, located in the north island of the nation, has a special and spiritual importance for the Māori people.

The New Zealand Parliament has just passed a bill which gives the river the ability to represent itself through human delegates, one appointed by a Māori community, known as Iwi, and one by the Crown government.

The new status of the Whanganui River, or Te Awa Tupua, is believed to be unique in the world.

The Māori people recognize the river as part of the living mountains and the sea. Chris Finlayson, who negotiated the treaty, said the Whanganui Iwi had fought for recognition of the people's relationship with the river since the 1870's;

"Te Awa Tupua will have its own legal identity with all the corresponding rights, duties and liabilities of a legal person. I know some people will say it's pretty strange to give a natural resource a legal personality, but it's no stranger than family trusts, or companies, or incorporated societies."

When we consider an organization as a living entity with its own evolving purpose, it can be easier to invite individuals to separate their wants and needs from the wants and needs of the organization.

In this example, the river has two appointed representatives. In your company, everyone is invited to fill that role. Principles, ideas and values can be distilled into writing, but activating the organization as the holder of its own purpose requires *sensing* on the part of the team. It's a practice that moves beyond the merely intellectual to include imagination and intentional reflection.

In *Reinventing Organizations,* Frederic describes Evolutionary Purpose simply:

Instead of trying to predict and control the future, members of the organization are invited to listen and understand what the organization is drawn to become, where it naturally wants to go.

At the end of this chapter we provide a series of exercises to help you tune into your organization's unique and evolving purpose.

Perspectives on Purpose

Purpose is a declaration of meaningful ways a team chooses to use its time; the place where **intent, being** and **doing** come together. Most importantly, it's *not* a description of a company's value proposition or a snazzy marketing slogan. Finding and articulating a clear, actionable purpose that creates alignment is incredibly challenging.

Personal purpose for the founders precedes uncovering organizational purpose. Having some level of clarity and certainty about your unique purpose, vocation and calling comes first. The leader then becomes a steward for organizational meaning.

Understanding whether you have found meaningful work is the first step in leading with purpose. How much do the following statements resonate as true for you?

- I have a good sense of what makes my job meaningful.
- I know my work makes a positive difference in the world.
- My work helps me better understand myself.
- I understand how my work contributes to my life's meaning.
- I view my work as contributing to my personal growth.
- My work helps me make sense of the world around me.
- The work I do serves a greater purpose.

In her paper, "The Power of Purpose: How Organizations are Making Work More Meaningful," Alison Alexander suggests developmental engagement as an approach for illuminating the connection between purpose and work. In Alison's words, purpose resides in the place "where a company aims to activate and develop more fully its employees (and the organization in general) to produce greater value for business and society."[4] The invitation here is to look to where personal development is pulling you and your colleagues.

Thoughts on Purpose

"Purpose is a central, self-organizing life aim that stimulates goals, manages behaviors and provides a sense of meaning. Purpose directs life goals and daily decisions by guiding the use of finite personal resources. Instead of governing behavior, purpose offers direction just as a compass offers direction to a navigator; following that compass (i.e., purpose) is optional."[3]

– Dr. Patrick McKnight and Dr. Todd Kashdan

Kazimierz (Kaz) Gozdz, a founding member of the Society for Organizational Learning, describes a similar approach to unearthing an organization's hidden purpose. Kaz's approach honors the strong visionary sense held by many founders.

What does the leader dream of doing differently, of changing, of inventing? The journey of strategic discovery, innovation or breakthrough begins with the foreknowledge of hidden implications, which the team's discovery will reveal. This foreknowledge can result from the need to solve a vexing problem or pursue an opportunity, and it gives rise to an irrepressible impulse to leap into the unknown. The discovery of a high challenge catalyzes passionate purpose—a calling—the impulse to create and pursue the hidden meaning.

For some, the concept of purpose is too soft and nebulous. If that's the case for you, think about your company "promise" instead. Social-innovation design pioneer Cheryl Heller defines a company's promise as, "The commitment a business makes to each of the people who interact with it. It's a promise that defines what is unique about the company and what people will get for their money and their time, whether they are a customer, partner, investor or employee."[5] In every purpose statement there is an implicit promise. The invitation is to make that promise more explicit.

Examples of Purpose

Articulating authentic purpose brings energy and focus to a team. It acts as a gravitational force for people sharing a similar sense of purpose. Below are examples of purpose statements. On first read they may seem somewhat superficial or uninspiring. Not until we dig into the essence of the companies do we experience the difference between a purpose statement and true purpose.

TOMS: "We believe we can improve people's lives through business."

TOMS is most known for its commitment to give a new pair of shoes to an impoverished child each time it sells a pair of shoes. The company's purpose originated from founder Blake Mycoskie's personal experiences while traveling and volunteering in Argentina.

Decurion Corporation: "To provide places for people to flourish."

Decurion Corporation operates subsidiaries ranging from entertainment centers to senior living facilities and commercial real estate. The organization is committed to the belief that profitability and human development can emerge as one, and it works to enact this belief at every level of its businesses. As a result, it is defined more by why it exists and how it operates than by its commercial portfolio. Believing business is a place for people to flourish, Decurion espouses many self-management principles. One example is a ten-week course offered to employees called "The Process of Self-Management" which includes exploring personal purpose, skillful speech and servant leadership.

Southwest Airlines: "To connect people to what's important in their lives through friendly, reliable, and low-cost air travel."

Southwest is one of the most cited examples of a corporation successfully living its purpose. The company was started based on one simple notion: "If you get your passengers to their destinations when they want to get there, on time, at the lowest possible fares, and make darn sure they have a good time doing it, people will fly your airline."[6] Almost 40 years later, the airline continues to embody this purpose and thrives as a result.

Crisp: "To enable consultants to be happy."

Crisp was founded in 1999 by consultants, for consultants. In their own words, "We are not a regular consulting company. We have no CEO and no managers. All consultants are self-employed." The Crisp team released their unique operating model as open source reference.[7]

Does your organization have a documented purpose? Does it still hold true today? Does it reflect and integrate the values and individual life purposes of the team? Is it something you talk about and reflect on regularly? How would it feel to realize it has changed, evolved and is no longer reflective of the organization?

Exercises To Stimulate Thinking

The process of unearthing your purpose begins by asking and answering questions until a coherent message begins to emerge. This may take months or even years. Personal and organizational purpose blends throughout the process. The following exercises are offered as potential starting points.

Exercise: Start Uncovering Your Personal Purpose In Five Minutes

In his TED talk, Adam Leipzig walks his audience through five simple questions.[8] The same questions can be applied personally or to your organization as a whole. The answers need not be any more complex than the questions.

Question 1: Who are you?
Question 2: What do you love to do?
Question 3: Who do you do it for?
Question 4: What do those people want or need?
Question 5: How will they change or transform as a result of what you give them?

Exercise: Who, Why And How Does Your Organization Serve?

The folks at the research and consulting firm Imperative have a brilliant worksheet that guides organizations through three critical decisions. By forcing a decision on each of these three questions, your purpose will begin to take shape.

Question 1: Who does our work have the greatest impact on? (Choose one)

- Our greatest impact is on Society.
- Our greatest impact is on Organizations.
- Our greatest impact is on Individuals.

Question 2: Why is our work necessary? (Choose one)

- Our work is necessary to ensure a fair and level playing field for everyone.
- Our work is necessary to remove barriers that keep people from reaching their full potential.

Question 3: What is our core competency? (Choose one)

- Our core competency is creating communities and connections.
- Our core competency is addressing issues that people face.
- Our core competency is uncovering knowledge and information to share with others.
- Our core competency is building systems that are able to continually create remarkable results.

Exercise: Four Hard Questions To Ask About Your Company's Purpose

In their 2016 Harvard Business Review article, Dominic Houlder and Nandu Nandkishore provide four excellent questions to use in testing your organization's purpose. The following quotes come from that article.[10]

Question 1: Is your purpose specific enough to defend?

"Statements of purpose often float upward into fluffy, generic moral injunctions, or land heavily as marketing slogans and value propositions."

If your purpose is not specific enough yet, try parsing it down to smaller core elements. Your purpose evolves over time. Go for specificity over the generic.

Question 2: What's fixed and what's up for grabs?

"Assuming that purpose is fixed for all time is a big mistake—only a generic purpose can be unchanging."

What elements of your purpose will you fix for now until a need to evolve emerges?

Question 3: What's your plan for defending your purpose despite short-term temptations?

"Short-term pressures are inevitable. How will you plan for them, and plan to protect your organization's purpose despite them?"

You may be doing this already, perhaps without being aware. These are often your non-negotiables; the things you feel so strongly about that you won't waiver.

Question 4: Is the organization's purpose connected to your own?

"...you are the channel for your organization's purpose; if it fails to connect with you, it can hardly connect with others."

Continuing the Journey

The ability to clearly articulate your purpose is different from knowing your purpose. Both parts may take time. The best you can do is articulate what you believe to be true today. It may not be sufficient over the long-term but it's a foundation from which you can build.

The purpose journey is a balance between reflection and action. Over time you are likely to find yourself toggling back and forth between certainty and doubt. Refinements will emerge with new information and changing circumstances.

Chapter 4

CREATING THE STRONGEST TEAMS

THE NECESSITY OF PSYCHOLOGICAL SAFETY AND HOW TO FOSTER IT

Let's say you wake up tomorrow as a new member of an established team. This team is filled with people who have been around the block a few more times than you. From the outset, the team leader starts shooting down your ideas. Your good work goes unnoticed while every mistake is called out in front of your colleagues.

How do you respond? At first, you might push back. Or grin and bear it, hoping it's simply posturing or a test. But it doesn't stop, it intensifies. Your frustration increases as does your quiet resentment of the team leader and, by extension, the entire team for their silent complicity.

Before long you begin second-guessing your every decision, fearful your place on the team is in jeopardy—maybe even your job. All you can think about is protecting yourself. With this as your mindset, the quality of your contributions decline. Eventually you leave.

This scenario plays out in teams everywhere.

The leaders of Google became curious about why some teams within their organization excelled while others floundered. Committed to understanding the "secret sauce" of a flourishing team, Google began a comprehensive study. After examining the performance of 180 teams, the researchers were stumped. "We had lots of data, but there was nothing showing that a mix of specific personality types or skills or backgrounds made any difference. The 'who' part of the equation didn't seem to matter."[1]

The researchers persevered until they eventually found a strong correlation. They discovered the level of psychological safety within a team is the number one determinant of how successful and productive the team will be. When there is a shared belief that the team is safe for interpersonal risk-taking, team performance improves. In contrast, as seen in the scenario above, when team dynamics lead individuals to feel unsafe, team performance declines. In the simplest terms, how we treat our colleagues is directly related to how our teams perform.

---

*Psychological Safety: a shared belief that the team is **safe** for interpersonal risk taking.*

As the researchers dug deeper, they found two specific behaviors present in teams with high psychological safety. These same behaviors are missing in other teams. In high performing teams, all team members speak in roughly the same proportion. Some voices may be more dominant for any given topic, but in the end, everyone is heard.

Secondly, stronger teams have the ability to sense how others are feeling by tuning into tone of voice, body language and other social cues. This enables the team to monitor its own emotional health.

Here is the honest reflection from a member of an organization in New Zealand who craves more of these behaviors in her team:

> *I often struggled to operate within the bounds of this working group which I've distilled down to two learnings:*
>
> *1) Lack of whanaungatanga (Māori for "like family" relationships) amongst the group. There needs to be a level of trust created, which takes time and generosity and is more than "the work."*
>
> *2) Lack of kawa (or "how our small group chooses to be with one another"). I often felt muted in our meetings, with concepts and language inaccessible for me and no clear way "in" to the group dialogue.*
>
> *Both kawa and whanaungatanga assist me in understanding the edges of things which results in me feeling safe, confident and able to work well with others. Without these, the cracks are less forgiving, intentions are forgotten, and people can feel backed into a corner, which I think, in part, is what is going on here.*

A heightened focus on psychological safety is necessary in a company's scale-up phase—when teams need to learn fast while working in a complex, changing environment. When people cannot talk about their challenges openly and instead feel the need to protect their image as competent contributors, there is little room to learn and grow individually and as a team.

Psychological safety is built on trust. You need to trust that being vulnerable and taking social risks will not result in judgement or negative repercussions. We all share a deep desire to be valued and respected as individuals and team members.

Psychological safety is especially important when success depends on the **creativity and rate of learning experienced by the team as a whole**, not just of the individuals. However, it's important to recognize that psychological safety isn't a team "skill," it's an environmental condition.

Elements of Psychological Safety

Transparent Learning

When situations are framed as learning opportunities, there is a greater willingness to run the risk of looking ignorant, intrusive or negative.

Leaders create the conditions for a psychologically safe environment by welcoming opinions (including dissent) on goals and strategies from any and all colleagues. Experiment with the following to model a more open, safe environment where mistakes and errors are shared as opportunities for learning.

"Based on this experience, let me share what I learned."

"I learned something today I'd like to share so you can benefit and avoid a similar mistake."

"I screwed up and I learned in the process."

Increased psychological safety can be conflated with decreased accountability. These are two independent factors. High safety and high accountability can and should co-exist within the team. This combination drives learning and positively impacts motivation. An environment can be safe for sharing mistakes while still setting a high expectation for performance. For example, you can expect your colleagues to perform well, share their learning for everyone's benefit, and take ownership for ensuring their mistakes get fixed. This can be done without placing blame.

Brainstorming & Psychological Safety

"Brainstorming sessions often demonstrate how easy it is to shut down free-flowing ideation—the literal opposite outcome than what was intended. Before our colleague can finish explaining her idea, we instinctively run the idea through our internal filters, compiling a mental list of why the idea won't work. We often place too much value on past experiences and become wrapped up in our own thoughts. As a result we fail to give sufficient air time to other alternatives."

– Brent

Teams that excel work hard to stimulate idea generation as a way to learn. When an individual's idea gets replaced by a better one, the previous idea is valued as a discussion starter.

Next time you sense yourself or others shutting down new ideas or narrowing in on one idea too quickly, experiment with your own version of the following language.

"Let's challenge ourselves to build on that idea and see what we can learn."

"Can I propose an alternative to play with for a few minutes?"

"Admittedly, I'm pretty excited about my idea. That said, I'd like you to challenge me on it to see what I can learn in the process. Perhaps something better will come up."

Inclusivity

Some people are comfortable and confident speakers who think fast and debate effectively. Others are not. **Often the extroverts, experts and elders do most of the talking.** The knowledge and experience of quieter members isn't considered because it's rarely heard. New group members and those with less experience can offer valuable, fresh insights. Every member of the team shares in the responsibility of ensuring balance within conversations.

Next time you are in a conversation or meeting where voices are not equally represented, experiment with calling it out and inviting participation.

"Now that we've heard Sam's perspective, I'd love to hear what others are thinking about this topic."

"Ellie, we haven't heard from you for a bit. I'm curious what you think about this?"

"Before we close out this topic, let's do a quick round table check-in. In one or two sentences, let's share where each of us is at."

"I've been talking for a while. Let me stop and see what you are thinking about this. Do you agree or do you have other ideas we should explore?"

"I'm noticing that three of us are doing most of the talking. Let's give everyone else a few minutes to chime in with other ideas."

Team Coherence

Coherence is defined as the integration of diverse elements, relationships or values—otherwise known as "fit" and "alignment." Often the sense of coherence, or lack thereof, plays out in team meetings. It's not unusual for a fast moving, fast growing team to have overly full agendas during meetings. The pressure can lead everyone in the meeting to push through the agenda despite signs the team is not in agreement or aligned. Trust and safety slowly degrade as a result.

For meetings requiring formal agendas, some teams build in space for interpersonal connection. This can take the form of an initial check-in, which we explore further in Chapter 10.

Throughout meetings, when a team member believes their colleague needs a chance to be heard, they call it out and make space.

To help prioritize coherence over efficiency, experiment with the following:

- Before moving to a new agenda item or wrapping up the meeting, try asking, "Does anyone have any lingering tensions?"
- Important emotional cues can get missed when things move too quickly. Make a conscious effort to tune into emotional cues. Does the nod of a head *really* mean the other person is on board with what is being said?

Supporting Your Team's Psychological Safety

There is no secret sauce to building psychological safety within your team. The goal is to continue experimenting with rituals that encourage and support interpersonal risk-taking. Here are a few more approaches to try.

- **Lead by example** – Your team will be more confident in taking social risks if they see you doing the same. Be vulnerable. Share your mistakes—the bigger, the better. Have fun with it. Add some humor.

- **Get personal** – Share something personal with your team that wouldn't otherwise come up in day-to-day business conversation. Traditional workplaces prioritize the rational part of the human experience and discount the emotional, intuitive and spiritual parts. By getting personal, you show your team all components of being human are seen as valuable elements of business.

- **Create a shared experience** – At the core of psychological safety is respectful and supportive human-to-human communication. This level of communication becomes easier the more we know each other at a deeper level. A team barbeque, hike or evening out for drinks creates the opportunity for relationship-building that stretches beyond day-to-day work.

- **Become curious** – Next time you are inclined to judge someone on your team, choose to become curious instead. Ask questions. Become interested in how and why they are delivering results different from what you'd hoped to see.

- **Ask for feedback at the end of tough conversations** – Relaying difficult messages is, well, difficult. If you find yourself delivering some tough love to a colleague, ask for feedback at the end: "It was challenging for me to deliver this message to you. I would appreciate some feedback on

Psychological Safety in Action

"Brent, Travis and Susan come from diverse backgrounds and have different life experiences. While sharing many of the same values when it comes to building progressive and successful workplaces, they hold differing opinions on how to best convey certain ideas. While writing *Reinventing Scale-Ups,* discussions usually ended in alignment around one person's opinion, or evolved into a blended solution.

One area where they haven't come to agreement is around the use of anonymous surveys, particularly when measuring psychological safety.

Susan believes anonymous surveys are antithetical to progressive workplaces and that anything needing to be measured is better surfaced via interpersonal discussions. For her, the type of environment engendered by anonymously airing grievances goes against our main assertions about the value of transparency.

Brent and Travis see anonymous surveys as a valuable tool for gathering data quickly and identifying core issues within an organization. They believe this approach is helpful, even within organizations which deeply value and practice transparency.

Although the three disagreed, there was enough inclusivity and coherence to allow both ideas to flourish. Through collaboration and creativity, a third way of presenting the ideas evolved without having to silence either voice. To me, this was a fantastic example portraying psychological safety in action and how it can result in tangible benefits."

– Nicole, Editor

how my message was received. Is there something I could have said or done differently that would have been more helpful to you?" This type of ask shows that you genuinely care about the other person and demonstrates your vulnerability in the process.

Fostering psychological safety is a team-wide responsibility. It takes time to build and can erode quickly. As a leader within the business, one of your most impactful roles is the creation and maintenance of an environment where everyone feels valued.

Chapter 5

ADULT-TO-ADULT RELATIONSHIPS

AGREEMENTS, ACCOUNTABILITIES AND COMMITMENTS THAT WORK

Traditional companies operate under the assumption that managers know best and should therefore be in charge. As we outlined in Chapter 2, authority can quickly turn into power. These power-based environments mirror many characteristics of adult-child relationships, where permissions must be granted and consequences doled out. **If the quality of relationships within our organizations determines the effectiveness of our work, then hierarchies place limits on that effectiveness.**

What if, instead, your organization was built on a strong foundation of healthy adult-to-adult relationships? Successful self-managed teams rely on such relationships and the agreements, commitments and accountabilities they support.

Commitments

"Commitment-making and commitment-keeping are critical self-management skills. There is history and research around the concept of commitment-keeping. Commitments are affirmative speech acts. Commitments have structure and a life cycle. Commitments are one of the most misunderstood and dysfunctional concepts in the life of most organizations. A major problem in many (if not most) organizations is that people can be sloppy about the way they make and fulfill commitments, resulting in suboptimal levels of trust, excessive frustration and major disappointment. Trust flows from proven integrity, which flows from effective commitment keeping and communication."[1]

– Doug Kirkpatrick
Author of *Beyond Empowerment: The Age of the Self-Managed Organization*

Social Contracts

In their HBR article, Christine Riordan and Kevin O'Brien identify social contracts as a critical first step in turning a group of employees into a great team.[2] Social contracts provide the distribution of authority that allows the entire team to feel a sense of ownership. The term "social contract" may seem foreign, but your team already has many of these contracts in place. They are the sometimes documented but often unspoken ways things get done within the group. Are people expected to be on time for meetings or is it normal to be late? Can team members openly disagree with their leader or is doing so taboo? Are working hours fixed or flexible?

Social contracts, formal or otherwise, create mutual understanding—for better or worse. When created consciously, they provide the solid foundation upon which a team's ability to trust and be open with one another is built. Social contracts in this spirit foster learning and inclusivity, leading team members to feel:

> *I belong here. I understand what it means to be part of this tribe. I can maintain my uniqueness while contributing to this team.*

Co-created Agreements and Social Contracts

Traditional companies use employment contracts, job descriptions and policies as tools to articulate expectations and control activities. Often the content of these documents does little to inspire proactive team engagement and goes unreferenced until troubles arise. Social contracts offer a better option.

Effective social contracts are different from typical policies in two key ways:

1. They define formal relationships and agreements between a member and the group, not just between a member and their leader.
2. These agreements are adjusted and customized whenever needed to evolve with the group.

Often, social contract documents are living, breathing artifacts anyone can amend through a pre-agreed process. The agreements are published, easily accessible and editable. They take different styles and formats, and may go through a periodic updating process sometimes referred to as *refactoring*.

Refactor

"Refactor is a metaphor from software development. It's something programmers do after they've been working on a piece of software for a while and they've developed a better understanding of how it should be working. They clean up how it functions internally to make it simpler, more readable, better performing and easier to change and improve later—usually without radically changing its functionality or reason for being. In software, refactoring is a way to fix technical debt."

– Alanna Irving

The same rules on refactoring apply to the hygiene of a company's culture. Continually refactoring the core pieces of culture helps bring closure to elements that are no longer working well. It's not always about adding "new features" to improve specific cultural problems. Sometimes simplifying is equally important.

The documents we are outlining here differ from traditional human resource policy handbooks. HR handbooks tend to be legalistic, focusing on compliance. The language of these documents is "command and control." The content gets pushed "down" into the organization.

The style we are suggesting has a different feel. One of the earliest examples comes from the gaming software company Valve. The Valve Handbook was one of the first public handbooks to outline the look and feel of working in a leaner, more self-managed style.[3] It's an operating manual of sorts that has been inspirational to many organizations looking to move beyond a traditional list of policies to a more supportive, human approach.

Another example of this innovative style is that of the organization Enspiral. Enspiral is a collective of social entrepreneurs focused on supporting people working on meaningful issues. They go beyond basic social contracts to co-create agreements for everything from how money gets spent to how diversity is fostered—all documented in their open source handbook.[4] Enspiral's handbook took shape based on the need to capture the loose arrangements and assumptions already in place. Through rigorous discourse and consent, the team processes decisions and documents the resulting agreements.

Some organizations have roles or groups responsible for creating team-wide agreements. In this case, the agreements need to be made available to the entire organization for discussion, reflection and amendment *before* they're adopted.

Agreements only work when they are transparent to everyone involved and, ideally, co-created. How can I be accountable to an agreement I haven't seen, don't remember, didn't commit to or can't reference?

Capturing and recording those agreements can make the social contracts in your organization more visible and concrete. Try choosing an unwritten, implicit agreement that's working well in one part of your organization and co-create an organization-wide social contract. For example, if one team has adopted an effective meeting practice or decision-making approach, consider documenting and sharing it as the foundation for a new

"Some of the decisions we make at Enspiral are easy, some are incredibly challenging and emotionally demanding. We are a community that values dissenting voices and the conditions required to hold that in a generative rather than reductive manner requires a lot of care and consideration. Recently I had the experience of making a proposal for a change in governance which would have delegated some aspects of decision-making to a small group of members. I was prepared for dissenting voices, but I wasn't prepared for my proposal to be blocked, which it was. In hindsight that was the right decision, but at the time I really struggled. I felt that I had failed to adequately convey the intention of my proposal. In reality, there was a fundamental flaw in my thinking and only because of our culture of encouraging and honoring dissenting voices was I able to accept the outcome without feeling personally aggrieved."

– Susan

organization-wide agreement. In doing so, consider including the following:

- What exactly is the agreement you are proposing?
- How can everyone's voice be included?
- If there is an action as part of the agreement, who is responsible?
- If appropriate, how and when will this agreement and related progress be tracked?
- Is there a specific timeframe associated with this agreement or will it become an ongoing part of team expectations?
- How and when will new people to the organization be introduced to this social contract?

Individual Social Contracts

In self-managing organizations, co-created social contracts between colleagues form the basis of how work gets done. An often referenced example is the Morning Star Colleague Letter of Understanding (CLOU).[5] The CLOU is a document created by each team member in collaboration with his or her team.

Each CLOU includes:

- A Personal Commercial Mission (PCM) where the author defines their fundamental purpose within the organization.
- Key activities the author agrees to do in pursuit of their PCM.
- Stepping stones, or key measures, by which the author will assess their own performance.
- Time commitments (a self-set due date).
- A list of CLOU colleagues affected by the commitments who sign off on the document.

Day-to-day Commitments

Social contracts also apply to day-to-day interactions. Each time we make an agreement with a colleague—to send a file, finish a project by a certain time or make an introduction—we create a new social contract.

When we deliver as expected, we are meeting the terms of our social contract. The more we deliver on our commitments, the more trust we build. The opposite is also true—trust degrades with each missed commitment.

To reduce the impact of miscommunication in these more casual day-to-day agreements, experiment with your own version of these three habits:

Review: *"Before wrapping up, let's review the deliverables we each committed to so we ensure we're both on the same page."*

Recap: *"I'm going to send you a quick email recapping my takeaways from our meeting to ensure we are aligned. Can you reply to let me know if you agree or if I missed anything?"*

Record: *"Let's pop open a document and capture our conversation real-time."*

Accountability

If we aspire to agile, self-managing organizations, collective accountability is a necessary ingredient. Operating within adult-to-adult relationships means a sense of shared accountability needs to exist between all team members, not just with the leader. When a commitment is missed, the responsibility of renegotiation falls to those who failed in delivering on that commitment. Alternatively, the people impacted become responsible for having the necessary conversations directly and respectfully with the appropriate individuals.

When those conversations don't happen, leaders often take on the role of judging missed commitments and doling out consequences. In self-managing teams, the leader's role shifts to coach and facilitator. By coaching team members to solve their own problems and offering to act as a facilitator (but not judge) when needed, teams learn how to operate with shared accountability.

One great way to keep accountability alive, both yours and the team's, is to ritualize it. Here are three examples of accountability rituals to try:

1. A real or virtual whiteboard of agreements combined with a daily stand-up meeting to quickly review and reset agreements.
2. Beginning weekly meetings with an accountability review based on a running agreements log.
3. Using a shared communication tool such as Slack to share accountability updates, or go even further and use a bot to prompt for updates.

Handling the Misses

Commitments will get missed. If those misses don't get called out, a culture of regular commitment-breaking emerges. Responding to misses is tough. Our automatic reaction often gravitates to silence (ignoring the issue) or punishment (attacking or blaming). Neither approach solves the problem. Instead, they diminish trust and rob your team of a valuable development opportunity.

In these moments, your team has an opportunity to strengthen its relationship with accountability by having honest, respectful and timely conversations. In Chapter 9, we delve into the topic of feedback to help with these difficult discussions.

Your team is relying on your accountability. You will occasionally make mistakes and fail to deliver on your commitments. In a fast-paced environment you are stretched thin and reprioritize commitments hourly. To build a culture of accountability, acknowledge your misses and share what you will do differently in the future. Encourage your colleagues to hold you accountable and respect them when they do. Your team learns from both what you say and what you do. How you manage your own mistakes ripples through the organization.

Next time commitments start to slip, experiment with having a quick collective "accountability debrief" using these three questions:

1. What is the impact of this miss?
2. What caused the miss? (Not to blame or shame but to identify the issues.)
3. What's to be learned?

Two Pitfalls To Avoid

Making agreements and maintaining healthy levels of accountability are collective undertakings requiring an environment of transparency and relying on adult-to-adult discussion. Team function—and dysfunction—is contagious. Habits spread quickly, and ultimately stick. A conscious effort is required to avoid the following two pitfalls:

1. **Avoid having one person fall into the role of accountability enforcer.** Failing to do so locks that individual, usually the leader, into an unhealthy relationship dynamic within the team. Bypass this situation by experimenting with the rituals outlined above, and rotating roles.
2. **A second challenge is overextending oneself and missing commitments as a result.** At its core this pitfall reflects an inability to say no—to oneself and to others. In her work, Dr. Brené Brown has ritualized the mantra "choose discomfort over resentment." Leaders

guide their teams in prioritizing decisions and making uncomfortable choices.

Take Action

Here are some ideas to help embed agreements and accountability into your organization's DNA. Pick one or two and try them out.

1. Add an accountability checkpoint into an existing meeting.
2. Within the next week, have a conversation with someone who failed to keep a commitment. Practice seeking understanding and giving feedback without turning to shame or blame.
3. Have the team experiment creating simple CLOUs.
4. Create a physical or virtual whiteboard listing the most important and urgent team agreements.
5. Introduce a ten-minute standing meeting daily to review accountabilities from yesterday and reset for today.

If you have doubts about your team's ability to make and keep commitments, get curious. Why is that? Engage the team in conversation around the topic. Do others feel the same? Experiment with your own approaches to making commitments and holding others accountable. As your team's skills mature with respect to agreements, commitments and accountabilities, so will the healthy adult-to-adult relationships that define reinvented scale-ups.

Chapter 6

MATCHING STRENGTHS TO NEEDS

DEFINING ROLES AND RESPONSIBILITIES

Work needs to be done. You trust the members of your team to do that work. On the surface it's simple matchmaking. However, experience tells you the reality of organizational productivity is far more complex.

- Work goes undone.
- People fail to meet expectations.
- Task boredom sets in.
- Career aspirations require tending and don't always align with business needs.

It can be like trying to assemble a puzzle in which both the picture and the shape of the pieces keep changing.

What if there was a panacea for overcoming these challenges? Edwin Jansen at Fitzii, a 15-person (and growing) recruitment solution for small companies, believes there is. His answer: remove yourself from the role of matching people to jobs.

Leaders tend to play the role of Puzzle Assemblers. In most businesses the CEO acts as the Chief Puzzle Assembler. When there's a need for a new role, a leader defines it. When a team member struggles, a leader deals with it. When it's time for career growth, a leader determines how to make it happen.

The greatest challenge in this model is the inability of leaders to be mind readers. If only we could look deep into everyone's soul and extract the relevant information. What do they love to do? What do they do best? How are they motivated and demotivated? Unfortunately, busy leaders have neither the time nor supernatural ability required to sufficiently answer these questions.

In their book, *Primed to Perform*, Neel Doshi and Lindsay McGregor investigate how companies build the highest performing cultures.[1] They look at the following nine factors impacting employee motivation: performance reviews, governance processes, compensation, leadership, workforce and resource planning, community, career ladders, organizational identity and role design. In their words:

> *The most powerful and the most overlooked source of total motivation is the design of a person's role within an organization. Often, jobs are designed entirely around tactical performance. We have a strategy. We turn that strategy into a process. We then write a job description to execute that process. Rarely, however, do we craft a role that inspires total motivation and adaptive performance.*

Poorly designed roles can make it almost impossible to create a high-performing culture.

Still, leaders invest significant time working with incomplete information. They aim to match people and tactical work, unaware of the science of human behavior.

Over the last two years, Fitzii has adopted an approach they call the "Role Advice Process" or "RAP." Fitzii is self-managed and chooses to work without traditional management structures, so there is no one person responsible for designing roles or managing team performance. As a result, they need a way to work through role-based issues within a self-management scaffolding. The RAP has become a core element of how they operate as a company. Since being implemented, the process has had a dramatic impact on the team.

- One person who wasn't performing well put themselves on a three-month probation with the intention of either improving or leaving the organization. Along the way they discovered an entirely different role, in which they are now thriving.
- One person decided to split their time and salary with Fitzii's parent company that needed help on a project.
- Two team members chose to leave Fitzii after realizing their ideal roles didn't exist within the company.
- Everyone else who did the RAP made meaningful changes to their roles, experiencing increased impact and personal engagement.

In Edwin's words, "The Role Advice Process was voted our most effective practice by the team. It really is the closest thing to a panacea that I've ever seen in business. Got a people problem? Try a Role Advice Process."

In essence, the RAP is a way of crowdsourcing the design of a role. A broader set of opinions help align the needs of the business and the strengths of the individual. Think about your role for a moment. Could you increase your impact and engagement if you redesigned your role? Through the RAP, you define the set of tasks best aligned with your strengths and things you enjoy.

Does this mean you get to drop everything from your plate that you don't enjoy? It does not. At least not until someone else pulls those tasks into their role. Reflecting back on the puzzle analogy, the puzzle is complete when there are no holes. Holes can be filled in two ways. The first is to reshape the current pieces of the puzzle to fit. The second is to hire a new puzzle piece. If the perfect puzzle piece does not yet exist, someone needs to step up and fill that hole.

A Sample Role Advice Process

Step 1: Embark on a RAP

The process begins with an individual's desire for input into the design of their role. Sometimes it's prompted by the individual themselves. Other times, a colleague may suggest the individual initiate a RAP because they have noticed a significant problem or opportunity.

Step 2: Announce the Start of a RAP

The individual declares to the team they are starting a RAP. A simple email to the team or a posting on an internal message board kicks off the process. The message includes who will be consulted, an open invitation for any team members to contribute advice and the date the individual plans to present the results. Sharing results within one month is recommended.

Step 3: Invest Time Self-Reflecting

The individual answers the following questions:

- Why am I doing this advice process? What led to this?

- What are my strengths, talents and interests? Where are they best put to use?
- What contribution am I currently making to the team? What's working well? What could be better?
- Could I increase my impact by shifting or changing my role? In what ways, specifically? What could be gained? What could be lost? Who would assume current duties I'd like to hand off?
- How do I feel about this potential change? What am I worried about? Excited about? What are the pros and cons?

Step 4: Seek Advice from Others

The individual presents their self-reflection and seeks advice from at least three team members. Advice comes from those who receive a personal request as well as anyone who self-selects into the process following the initial announcement. This allows for contributions from any team member who believes they may have valuable input or may be impacted. The questions in step three can serve as good discussion starters.

Step 5: Make a Decision

Decision time. Taking all information into consideration, the individual decides what they think should happen next. This could include changing roles, altering the current role or even leaving the organization.

Step 6: Present Results

The individual shares the results of the process with his or her team by creating a summary document. The communication should include their personal reflections, advice received, thought process, decision, reasoning for the decision and transition plan.

Step 7: Take Action

In a fully self-managed organization, the final step is to execute on the transition plan. No further approvals are required. The individual driving the change is responsible for ensuring a smooth transition with his or her colleagues. Any significant changes in responsibility, compensation or employment status need to be fully documented before the change can take place. Compensation changes may require additional steps. We dig deeper into this topic in Chapter 11.

Experimenting with a Role Advice Process

If Fitzii's process feels too radical a shift from how your organization operates, you can customize the approach to work for your culture. Start slow and test drive variations. The key is to shift responsibility of constructing an optimal role from manager to team member.

One easy way to try out the suggested process is to pick someone on your team who you believe is due for a role shift. Perhaps they are unhappy. Perhaps the business need for their role has expanded or dwindled. Introduce them to the process above and invite (but not force) them to give it a test drive. Remove the announcement step since the broader team doesn't yet know about the process.

Work with your colleague to select a list of people to seek advice from. Have your colleague complete steps three through five. They can come back to you for step six once they've compiled a recommendation and together, you can finalize a decision. The final step can be adapted to your regular way of finalizing role changes.

Test it out a few times and see what happens.

A Different Perspective on the Concept of Roles

Similar to Fitzii, Percolab operates as a self-managed team and has its own process for managing roles. Percolab is an innovative 14-person consulting firm with deep expertise in co-designing the future of work, participatory management practices and collaboration. Their role process involves thinking about all the responsibilities necessary to allow the organization to meet its purpose. Those responsibilities are grouped together into roles.

Unlike traditional organizations where one person is mapped to one job, individuals at Percolab may hold multiple roles or groups of responsibilities, at the same time. There is a flow and adaptability to matching Percolab's purpose with individuals' passions and learning objectives.

Percolab's transition to this role-based structure is relatively new. After completing the initial transition, Percolab's founder, Samantha Slade, shared the following process.[2]

Identifying Company Roles

Every organization already consists of a set of roles. By observing what is needed for the organization to meet its purpose, these roles can be made explicit. At Percolab, Samantha put on her role-identifying hat for a few months. She honed in on daily life at the company by asking herself questions: *What is the team working on? What are people talking about? Where do confusions, roadblocks and tensions repeatedly occur?*

In all, 32 roles were revealed as necessary sets of responsibilities. Many were already owned by team members while others were unassigned. Samantha gave each one a placeholder title: Banker, Legal Protector, Video Producer and so on. This was done in an open and transparent process.

During this time, Samantha resisted the temptation to look outside the company for influences, focusing instead on what was needed for the Percolab team based on their own unique way of functioning.

Writing Roles into Being

Each of the 32 roles needed to be articulated in writing. This process was completed as a team, allowing their collective intelligence to emerge. The roles were created to include:

- Role title: clear and aligned to the culture
- Role purpose: a short statement
- Role accountabilities: tasks and decision-making authority
- Role metrics: specific indicators to help the team see if the role is being well-stewarded

The team agreed that each member would be responsible for writing four to five roles. They set up a wiki in which people inserted first drafts. For each role, two additional team members iterated the document forward using their wisdom and experience. Everyone on the team committed to reading all the roles at this point in the process.

Adopting and Attributing Roles

The team held a two-and-a-half hour workshop to attribute the roles to individuals. The workshop process went as follows:

- A short refresher on the purpose of roles.
- A check-in round to see how everyone was feeling heading into the exercise and to give space to any apprehensions.
- Small groups discussed and reviewed the roles relevant to that group with the intention of bringing back to the team three proposals for improvements to the role drafts. Each of the proposals were processed using an **integrated decision-making process** (which we will explore in the next chapter).

Percolab Role Example

- Title: Banker
- Purpose: Reduce financial stress of all members of the collective, collaborators and organizations with whom we have transactions.
- Accountabilities:
  - Based on laws and obligations, foresee financial provisions and make and document all necessary payments to the government.
  - Act as contact for Percolab with the government, documenting key information, exchanges and situations.
  - Emit checks, once documentation is duly completed and, if appropriate, approved.
  - Inform members if a difficult financial situation arises and work through it openly and collectively.
- Metrics:
  - Financial stress of members is low—collective average rating of no more than two out of ten each month.
  - Payments are made within 30 days.
  - No penalties or interest to the government.

- An implementation date for the new role system was discussed and agreed upon.
- The roles were then attributed to individuals through a multi-step process.
  - The name of each role was written on an index card and laid out before the team.
  - Team members then individually wrote on the cards who they thought was best situated for stewarding that role. Including his or her own name was not allowed.
  - The group reviewed the collective perspective that had been revealed. Then, each person proposed two roles he or she had energy to steward. The group let the person know if there were any objections. If none, the roles were considered attributed.
  - A second round was then completed.
  - In a final round, anyone could propose anyone else for the remaining roles. Again there was a quick check for any opposition until all roles were attributed.
- Lastly, a closing round was completed allowing everyone to share their thoughts and feelings leaving the workshop.

Both the Fitzii and Percolab approaches remove the responsibility from the leader of playing match-maker between people and roles. In both cases, the team benefits from the insights of individual members and everyone has an opportunity to opt-in to work that feels meaningful. Undoubtedly these two approaches are not perfect and may not be right for your circumstances. The invitation we offer is to experiment beyond the tradition of defining comprehensive and static job descriptions. Instead, try releasing yourself from the responsibility of Puzzle Assembler by allowing the team to participate in a collaborative process.

Chapter 7

HOW TO DECIDE

DECISION-MAKING UNLEASHED

How are decisions made in your organization? Is there a single, planned approach? Or are there as many ways as there are people in the company?

Despite the critical role decision-making processes play in business, the topic receives little consideration. For agile and self-managed teams, a consistent, purposeful decision-making process is essential. It's a protocol that needs to be a standing agreement to ensure safe, transparent and effective teamwork.

Two decision-making methods tend to rule most organizations. These methods, or versions thereof, fall on opposite ends of a spectrum. At one end, leaders dominate by making decisions, then telling their teams how to implement those decisions. At the other end, teams become paralyzed as they try to reach consensus, or they appear to reach consensus only to later fail to support the decision. Neither of these approaches meet the need to quickly make definitive decisions everyone embraces in order to move forward with collective action.

Both speed and effectiveness can be achieved. Percolab utilizes a process called "Generative Decision-Making" (described in detail below). Their record is 19 quality decisions in 60 minutes.

Your team will be best served by aligning around a decision-making approach that fits your unique circumstances. However you choose to experiment, we recommend keeping the following in mind:

- Invest in educating all members of the organization on the way(s) the team makes decisions.
- Clearly articulate the decision-making approach you will use before heading into the process of making a decision.
- Over time, aim to adopt a single approach everyone understands to be the default process for your organization.

Making Decisions by Consent

There are two decision-by-consent approaches we've seen work well: the Advice Process and the Integrated Decision-Making Process.

Making decisions by consent enables team members to proceed in any area not otherwise assigned to an individual or role. It requires a team-wide agreement on how individuals will go about making those decisions. With this approach, decisions are generally led by those with domain accountability. Note that this is not decision-making by *consensus*, which requires each team member be consulted and confirm support in advance of a decision being finalized.

The Advice Process

The Advice Process declares one person as the *owner* of a particular decision. This is most often the person who recognizes a problem requiring a solution or the one who has related accountability. The owner seeks input and advice from two groups: individuals affected by the decision and subject matter experts.

It is assumed that people trust their colleagues to make decisions in the best interest of the collective, and individuals' input will be sought when appropriate. After seeking input, the decision owner proceeds in a way they feel is best for the organization. They do not need to act on all advice provided. Seeking approval or announcing their decision in advance of acting is not required. This approach elicits a sense of personal responsibility that leads to increased engagement.

The Advice Process relies on the power of adult conversation. The bigger the decision, the wider the net needs to be cast for additional advice. For small decisions, one additional perspective may be all that's needed. At times, advice from external advisors, industry experts or board members may be appropriate.

The Decision Maker by Dennis Bakke is a quick read and does an excellent job of explaining this process in detail.[1] He outlines how leaders who have traditionally filled the role of prime decision maker now become the ones choosing who is best positioned to be a decision owner in a given situation.

When done well, the Advice Process brings to life the true essence of self-management.

Using an online tool like Loomio[2] or CloverPop[3] can bring speed and transparency to the Advice Process. These tools are also excellent for making decisions in distributed teams.

Integrated Decision-Making Process

In comparison to the Advice Process, Integrated Decision-Making is a more structured approach. It's a tool normally used in a live meeting where everyone relevant to the decision is present.

How Poor Implementation of the Advice Process Kills Trust

"The Advice Process can backfire if misapplied. I worked with an organization grappling with a market-driven product change. As a result of the change, the company needed a different set of skills than those held by the individual in the customer support role. An Advice Process was started. The product manager solicited advice from other members of the team, but consciously excluded the most impacted individual to avoid confrontation. This resulted in the person being told her skills no longer fit the role and that she should therefore leave the company. Trust was severely compromised across the entire organization.

A better approach would have been to include the individual in the process. The product manager should have given the individual all of the information and allowed her to identify possible solutions or alternatives."

– Susan

Two key elements make Integrated Decision-Making powerful. First, whoever makes the first proposal becomes the proposal holder. Their job is now to onboard and integrate feedback from all other meeting participants. This process may result in a decision that diverges completely from the initial proposal.

Second, participants may only object to a proposal if they feel it will "cause harm or move us backward." Having a better idea is not a sufficient reason to object. This is where traditional consensus-based processes often fail. When individuals believe a better solution exists, the search for consensus can drag on endlessly. **Integrated Decision-Making operates on the agile principle of "good enough for now, safe enough to try."**

In Chapter 14 we will explore a business operating system known as Holacracy. Integrated Decision-Making is a core element of that system and includes six steps.[4]

1. **Presenting a proposal** – Anyone can start the process by describing a problem and proposing a solution, making them the *proposal holder*. If not already assigned, someone volunteers to facilitate the decision-making process and removes themselves as an active contributor to the decision.

2. **Inviting clarifying questions** – Anyone can ask the proposal holder clarifying questions. The proposal holder provides an answer to the question or states that an answer has not yet been contemplated. No reactions or dialogue are permitted at this point.

3. **Initiating a reaction round** – One-by-one, each person (except the proposal holder) has an opportunity to react to the proposal as they see fit. No additional discussions are permitted.

4. **Amending and clarifying** – The proposal holder can choose to clarify or amend the proposal based on what was heard in the last two steps. Once again, no discussion is permitted.

5. **Initiating an objection round** – The facilitator invites objections by asking each person in turn, "Do you see

any reasons why adopting this proposal would cause harm or move us backwards?" If no objections surface, the proposal is adopted.

6. **Integrating objections** – The goal of this step is to craft a proposal free of valid objections while still addressing the proposer's problem. The proposal owner focuses on each objection, one at a time. Once all objections are integrated into a new proposal, another objection round is completed. This process continues until a solution is adopted.

Both the Advice Process and Integrated Decision-Making Process may seem cumbersome and time consuming. With practice, they can quickly become the most efficient way to make decisions. As mentioned earlier, Percolab uses a decision-making process built on Integrated Decision-Making and has added additional interpersonal practices from the Art of Hosting.[5] They call it Generative Decision-Making.[6] With the whole team trained on the methodology, they can rapidly move through important decisions.

Many organizations create their own customized version of decision-by-consent. The distributed team at Enspiral uses the following principles to help them make better decisions:[7]

- Open multiple channels, online and in-person, to get well-rounded input.
- Involve people who are not in your geographical location and those you do not work with regularly.
- If you encounter tension, conflict or confusion, escalate communication to a higher bandwidth channel (Loomio to Slack, Slack to video, video to one-on-one, one-on-one to mediated discussion). Once resolved, report outcomes back to the group.
- Make conscious efforts to improve the experience for everyone (e.g. inviting in those not yet heard, clarifying

and summarizing points raised or suggesting good timing for a proposal).

In addition to consent-based decisions, we'll briefly mention two more traditional forms of decision-making and how to strengthen their effectiveness through experimentation.

Delegated decision-making is granting authority to individuals for specific types of decisions. This approach can be improved by increasing transparency within the organization before, during and after decisions are made. Sharing the thought process behind the decision and the major decision criteria used helps build trust and confidence within the team. The most common misuse of delegation is passing along decision-making responsibility without providing sufficient authority to execute on the resulting decision.

Consensus requires ongoing discussion until everyone involved agrees with the proposed solution or, at minimum, is prepared to support the decision. It requires a level of shared context that time often doesn't permit. This process can be especially useful when stakes are high, the decision is not reversible and most of the team shares sufficient context. The most common challenge is false consensus where individuals indicate a willingness to support and move on to other business, but are not actually aligned. The lack of consensus can show up later when some team members fail to fully support the decision or even sabotage it.

It's time to make some decisions about decision-making. Whatever path you choose for your organization, the first step is experimentation. To help you get started, here are a few questions to focus your exploration.

1. What's the current state of decision-making in your organization?
    a. Does your team make quick and effective decisions?
    b. How many decisions do you make unilaterally on

behalf of the company?

   c.   Does your organization have a single way of making decisions or many different approaches?

   d.   Are multiple decision methods creating confusion?

   e.   Is every new team member introduced to your organization's *specific and articulated* way of making decisions?

2.   How would you like decision-making to happen in your organization?

   a.   Can you envision having one primary decision-making approach? If not, why not?

   b.   What core principles do you believe should be part of every good decision-making process?

   c.   Do you want all big decisions made collectively?

   d.   Do you prefer to delegate day-to-day decision-making to the individual with the most context?

   e.   Should the individual who has accountability for the domain make decisions and own the outcomes?

   f.   Do you want to distribute the decision-making all the way to the edges of the organization? If not, why not? If so, how?

3.   If you would like to strengthen the quality and efficiency of decision-making in your business, what steps would you like to take?

   a.   What decision-making process would you like to try? (Reminder: Choosing a decision-making process is, in itself, a decision. Is it your decision to make or should the team participate in the choice?)

   b.   What upcoming decision offers a good opportunity for experimentation?

   c.   How will you ensure everyone involved in that decision understands how the selected decision-making process works?

How do you want to evolve decision-making in your organization? Pick an approach from above that feels most appropriate for your circumstances and give it a try. Effective decision-making can be a strategic advantage for scaling your business. Progress comes from experimentation and retrospective learning. Invest time now to reap benefits into the future.

Chapter 8

WORKING WITHOUT BLINDERS

BOOSTING TRANSPARENCY

Transparency is the secret to collapsing power hierarchies. It is the lifeblood of the self-managing organization. Transparency ensures everyone has the information required to fully and effectively contribute.

There are categories of information traditionally considered confidential. Salaries, margins and cash balances are a few examples. However, some organizations are beginning to appreciate the social cost of keeping information from the team and the missed opportunities of not distributing data and context.

Agile teams rely on multiple transparency-based tools and systems. Kanban boards,[1] software sprint boards[2] and burn down charts[3] are examples of physical artifacts used to make information visible and dispel assumptions. They provide the truth of what's going on – good, bad or ugly.

Despite the many benefits, it's easy to list arguments against transparency. Protecting the team from distractions and ambiguity is one frequently stated objection.

There is also the issue of trust. Many organizations simply haven't built enough trust to be comfortable sharing proprietary information, fearing it might fall into the wrong hands.

With knowledge comes power. When information is transparent, our sometimes fragile egos as leaders can come under threat. "If information isn't my source of power, what is?" We don't mention the fragility of ego to criticize but rather as an honest reflection of the human experience.

Our willingness to work transparently—or not—comes from our beliefs and the stories we tell ourselves. Are others capable of dealing with the ambiguity and anxiety often accompanying the "burden of knowledge?" Can the team have provocative conversations without getting distracted by information not immediately relevant? Does everyone on the team have the skill to manage confidential information appropriately?

100% transparency may not be achievable or appropriate. However, when in doubt, move towards sharing information.

Readiness for Transparency

To determine your readiness for introducing greater transparency, consider these statements as they apply to you and your organization:

- I believe our team can make better decisions by having more information.
- I believe the benefits of sharing information with the team outweigh potential risks.
- I believe people on our team are mature adults capable of managing the free flow of information.
- I believe I am capable of handling difficult conversations that arise from increased transparency.
- I recognize that holding information is a form of power which doesn't always serve our organization. I wish to reduce the amount of information we reflexively conceal.
- I'm prepared to tell our team what information, if any, will remain confidential and why.

When these statements feel more true than false, consider increasing transparency in your organization.

First Steps Toward Greater Transparency

Here are some guiding questions to help you map out practical next steps in experimenting with heightened transparency.

1. Whose decision is it to introduce more transparency into the organization? Is it a team decision or can you decide on your own?
2. How do you want to introduce greater transparency into your organization? By public proclamation? Quiet role modeling? Something in between?
3. What information is not currently shared within your organization but could be? Equity splits? Salaries? Revenue? Pricing levels? Fundraising amounts? Bank

balances? Source code? Product roadmaps?

4. How would you rank the sharing of this information from least risky to most risky?

5. What major benefits could come from sharing the information internally or more broadly? Building trust with stakeholders? Generating user input or content? Solving challenging problems? Creating a more empowered and committed team? Garnering positive PR?

6. What major risks might arise? How likely are those risks? How can they be minimized?

7. Based on the outcome of these questions, where can you start experimenting first?

Preparing for Potential Challenges

If you decide to start experimenting with increased transparency, here are some questions to ask yourself as the experiments unfold.

- Is a vocal minority keeping our organization from being more transparent? Not everyone may love the idea of transparency, for a variety of reasons. Remember, knowledge is power and some may struggle giving up that power.

- Am I recognizing when the team needs help interpreting data or putting it in context? Sometimes information needs to be broken down and shared in ways that reduce fear or frustration. For instance, sharing salaries openly before the team is ready or without first providing ample context is a recipe for disaster.

- Am I misattributing transparency as the root cause of problems that are emerging? Often transparency highlights issues which already existed covertly. Transparency gives way to productive—and challenging—workplace conversations on issues that might otherwise fester.

- Am I noticing the challenges but not the benefits of a more transparent workplace? We have a tendency to see negatives, especially when evaluating changes. Experiment with being more intentional in noticing positives. Appreciate that negatives often arise quickly while benefits can take much longer to materialize.

- Am I providing adequate time for improvements in the speed of decision-making and rate of team learning to emerge? Patience is required to allow the effects of new transparency in your organization to be realized.

- Am I being overly cautious? Fear is a powerful force. Will others steal my ideas? Will team members become demotivated by bad news? Can my colleagues handle the truth? These are all valid questions worth pondering. Often we allow irrational fear or over-stated concerns to outrank the benefits of transparency.

- Is information being shared frequently and fully? Data gets stale at an incredibly quick rate. Stale data can be worse than no data at all. The same can be said about partial data that leaves colleagues making assumptions to fill in the gaps. Teams keeping information free flowing at all times will outperform teams that are intermittently transparent.

Tools for Transparency

Here are some of our favorite tools for creating a more transparent workplace. Each allows entire teams to have visibility around the work-in-progress and real-time status of their colleagues' contributions.

The Google Suite of Tools – A powerful and easy way to share working documents. We wrote and edited this book together in real time from different places around the world using Google Docs.

Google Drive, Dropbox or Box – Great for sharing documents and files created in your organization.

Trello or Asana – Both are incredible tools for sharing and prioritizing work. We used Trello for coordinating our individual work while writing this book.

Slack or HipChat – Communication tools that can supplant email. One big advantage is the ability to add people to a thread allowing them to see conversation history while keeping their individual inboxes clear.

Loomio or CloverPop – Both programs make decision-making processes and their history more transparent.

Scrum or Kanban boards – Both are excellent for prioritizing work and making it broadly visible.

Keep in mind transparency is not about overwhelming colleagues with mass amounts of unnecessary and unhelpful data. It is about removing barriers to effective contributions and increasing psychological safety.

The team at SideFX recently implemented Slack as a tool for boosting efficient and effective communication. At first, the team used many "closed" channels, meaning conversations within a channel were available only to those specifically granted access. After some experimentation, the team decided to open most channels to full company access. The result? While participation in each channel remains relatively unchanged, everyone can now browse conversations at will to better understand what their colleagues are focused on. The sense of unnecessary secrecy has been removed.

Similarly, teams using video conferencing tools such as Zoom can record meetings and make those recordings available to the entire team. We will explore an example of this approach in Chapter 12 on Recruiting.

Is it time to name and challenge knowledge-based hierarchies in your organization? Take a step to increasing transparency. Then another. Then another. Before long transparency will become the norm within your team.

Chapter 9

BEING DELIBERATELY DEVELOPMENTAL

FEEDBACK AND REFLECTION

Giving and receiving quality feedback is a perennial challenge for individuals and organizations. Avoidance, hostility, passive-aggressive behavior and bullying are all examples of poor approaches to dealing with feedback. These habits are rife with negative impacts to the deliverer, the receiver and the organization overall.

Resistance to meaningful developmental conversations directly conflicts with behaviors of thriving scale-ups. When we leave our colleagues in a vacuum without clear feedback, learning stalls and often so does the company. On the other hand, blunt feedback can diminish psychological safety, often leading the receiver to withdraw from the team. It's a dilemma.

Rather than ignoring this challenge, an opportunity exists to ensure personal growth and development are defining components of your organization. Companies that do so are **deliberately developmental organizations (DDOs).**

What if we reimagine our workplaces as a source of opportunities to develop career capabilities while also nurturing empathy, authenticity and individuality?

In our professional lives, confidence, competence, rationality, strong problem-solving and other similar skills are traditionally prioritized.

Outside work, compassion, care, love, fun and related relationship-based dimensions are more in focus.

In reality, life outside our jobs provides opportunities to develop skills useful in our work. Similarly, work provides us opportunities to develop more fully as fulfilled, thriving individuals. This concept is embraced by DDOs. Robert Kegan and Lisa Laskow Lahey are the authors of *An Everyone Culture: Becoming a Deliberately Developmental Organization.* They outline three characteristics of DDOs:

1. Development is a specific, describable and detectable phenomenon.
2. Development has a robust scientific foundation.
3. Development has business value.

Kaz Gozdz from the Helix Group further defines these organizations as using business challenges as a natural curriculum for growing individual capacity. In doing so, organizational capacity is enhanced to address increasingly complex challenges. No training programs, no separate management process. Nothing extra. Personal capacity grows through the performance of daily tasks. Development is not limited to specific occasions or events, but is ongoing. In a DDO, everyone works on developing themselves, others and the organization everyday. Work is the primary context for this development with a culture of feedback being a core element.

> *"Ordinary organizations seldom make feedback a continuous experience, but even in organizations where feedback is frequent, the feedback strongly tends to be oriented to tracking and correcting behavior."*
>
> *– Lisa Laskow Lahey and Robert Kegan, An Everyone Culture: Becoming a Deliberately Developmental Organization*

Is it possible for everyone, on an ongoing basis, to deliver feedback that is useful, practical and compassionate? The traditional habit of companies amassing and delivering annual performance reviews suggests it is not. When feedback comes long after the optimal learning moment has passed, the benefit to the receiver is significantly diminished.

Try shortening the feedback cycle. For example, retrospectives in an agile environment ensure feedback occurs at the end of a two-week work sprint so the sharing is more timely, actionable and future-focused. Better yet, make feedback a reflexive, integrated practice.

Too often, behavioral feedback is used as punishment. Say an individual receives end-of-year feedback asserting that he is not a good listener. How unfortunate is it that the feedback wasn't provided in the moment so that the person in question could immediately work on changing their behavior? Thought leader Julian Stodd shares his thoughts on annual performance reviews:

> *Performance Reviews: still carried out annually, still trying to maintain some semblance of relevance, but generally used simply to control us, to prevent giving a pay raise, to come up with some trite list of "development activities" as if the organization has a better idea of what is needed than your community. In an age when learning is synchronous and co-created, when performance is judged and rated in the moment, absolutely nothing, not a single thing, is measured annually except our performance review.*

In a DDO, feedback is oriented not toward correcting an instance of behavior but toward shifting the mindsets that produced those behaviors. It's the difference between temporary changes made to please another and meaningful personal development.

Receiving Feedback

To be a good provider of feedback, we first need to be a respected receiver of feedback. How can we expect others to onboard feedback when we can't do the same ourselves? Learning and growth begin with an attitude of openness, curiosity and an assumption of good intent on the part of the feedback provider. Listening with gratitude comes through an appreciation that giving feedback requires taking a risk. Gratitude lowers our internal resistance to unexpected information, creating an environment where authentic communication becomes more natural. We retain the right to receive feedback as true and actionable, or merely as an interesting perspective for consideration.

If we build a healthy culture of feedback, it becomes easier to notice and welcome that feedback without becoming fearful or defensive. Just as the body builds muscle memory, this practice strengthens and becomes more reflexive over time.

Feedback as a Gift

"One of my favorite professors at Stanford Graduate School of Business often says, 'Feedback is a gift.' It's not always a gift we want. Sometimes it's a gift that we'd be happy to refuse. However, when we can root ourselves in the concept that there is something useful in this feedback, even if it's simply gaining a greater understanding of someone else's perspective, it can be much easier to approach all feedback with a sense of appreciation."

– Travis

Receiving Feedback Checklist

Consider how well you model the following behaviors. In which areas are you an excellent role model to your colleagues? Who could be a role model for you as you continue developing your skills as a receiver of feedback?

- I invite and encourage my colleagues to provide me with feedback.
- I notice when someone is trying to offer me feedback and create space for the feedback.

- I become curious about the feedback I am receiving and resist the urge to defend my choices or to dismiss the feedback as inaccurate.
- I choose a growth mindset by recognizing that feedback does not reflect on who I am as a person but on how I happened to show up at one particular moment.
- I show gratitude to the giver, irrespective of my agreement with the feedback.

The Basics of Giving Feedback

Diverse approaches and styles to providing feedback exist. *Radical Candor* by Kim Scott provides a simple philosophy well-suited to DDOs.[1]

Radical Candor

Popularized by Google and other large tech companies, *Radical Candor* teaches that steering clear of tough conversations has negative consequences. Avoiding feedback to protect feelings can be more damaging than a harsh critique. Challenging feedback—no matter how poorly given—creates the opportunity for change. Silence removes opportunity for growth.

Radical candor is composed of two components: **care personally** and **challenge directly**. The foundation of radical candor is a genuine concern for the other person and a desire to help them improve. The best way to help is to communicate your intentions directly. When someone knows you genuinely care, it is easier to accept direct and critical feedback.

In radical candor, and all good forms of feedback, the feedback goes directly to the person in question, not through an intermediary. You can leverage a coach or mediator, but at its core, the interaction is between the two people involved.

If you challenge directly but don't care personally, you've fallen into *Obnoxious Aggression*. This gets the information out there but puts the burden on the recipient to find value in the feedback despite emotional triggers the delivery might have created.

If you care personally but don't challenge directly, you've moved into *Ruinous Empathy*. You haven't given the receiver enough meaningful information about what they can correct. You're preventing their growth and development, likely for fear of damaging the relationship. This can easily lead to deferred and prolonged suffering.

If you neither care nor challenge, you're exhibiting *Manipulative Insincerity*. You're out for yourself and not for others or the company.

Radical candor is a powerful framework because this simple two-by-two **care-challenge** matrix is useful not just for giving feedback, but also for testing how feedback has been received.

Remember, feedback is measured at the receiver's ears. Ask recipients where on the grid they thought your feedback landed. In this way, you start to see your patterns and adjust your feedback approach when needed.

Here are a few good feedback tips to keep in mind, framed in the context of radical candor:

- Care Personally
    - Check your intention for sharing feedback—is it to amend the situation or is it an emotional reaction? Anchor in an intention of being helpful and initiating positive change.
    - Check to ensure the receiver is in an emotional state to absorb feedback by first asking permission to share your insights.
    - Offer feedback which incorporates the entire situation, including the positive aspects.
    - Relate the feedback to the other person's development goals.

- Challenge Directly
  - Frame feedback around specific behaviors and their impact on others, versus perceived intentions or personality traits.
  - Be detailed in outlining the situation, specific behavior and resulting outcome versus providing a generalized and inactionable critique.

An additional framework that complements Radical Candor is **Nonviolent Communication (NVC)**. As the name suggests, NVC is based on the principle of nonviolence. It assumes verbally or physically violent behaviors are learned defenses used to protect basic human needs. The Center for Nonviolent Communication describes this model in two parts: *empathetically listening* and *honestly expressing*. Within each part, there are four steps: observations, feelings, needs and requests.[2]

NVC emphasizes personal accountability for *our* feelings and compassion for the feelings of others. When someone's actions impact us, we are to take responsibility for honestly expressing that impact. In doing so, we also maintain a focus on empathetically listening to the underlying human needs of the other person. By articulating feedback in terms of our observations, feelings, needs and requests, defensiveness is reduced. When we define the impact we're experiencing without unnecessary generalization, or the use of emotionally-charged language, the receiver can more easily understand our concern. We can then move the discussion into a problem-solving mode.

To explore NVC in more detail, *Nonviolent Communication: A Language of Life* by Marshall Rosenberg is a helpful read.

Ritualizing Team Feedback

Ritualizing feedback practices in your culture encourages a growth mindset across the organization. Once your team has practiced feedback basics, consider experimenting with retrospectives.

No one knows the whole story of the project. Each person has a piece of the story. The retrospective ritual is the collective telling of the story and mining the experience for wisdom.[3]

Retrospectives

Retrospectives ritualize the practice of pausing to learn, often at the end of a project. The retrospective is a team meeting usually lasting between 30 minutes and two hours with a defined end time set in advance. The meeting focuses on making the next work segment more enjoyable and productive by both improving the processes the team uses and helping individuals develop.

David Horowitz is the CEO and co-founder of Retrium, a ten-person company providing software to simplify the retrospective process.[4] As you would expect, David and his team use retrospectives religiously and have discovered a series of side benefits as a result. Through repetition, the team built an indispensable set of skills related to process improvement and providing feedback.

Retrospectives range in scope and approach. In the early days of a company, a retrospective can be as simple as the founders going for a walk and discussing what they've learned. As the team grows and conversations become more dispersed, a more formal ritual becomes necessary.

On the formal side, Retrium offers four different approaches. Start, Stop, Continue is one example that works best with teams of five to fifteen people.

To begin, create three columns:

- Start (new things to try)
- Stop (things to eliminate)
- Continue (things that are working well)

Everyone on the team adds to each column until ideas stop flowing. The team then votes to narrow the list to one or two main areas of focus. Next, the group creates a way to measure improvements over the following two weeks. Lastly, someone is appointed to oversee these adjustments.

At the next retrospective, the team reviews progress. Other items from the last retrospective can be examined as a way to jumpstart the next cycle.

In a similar process, Start, Stop, Continue is replaced with four L's (Liked, Learned, Lacked and Longed For) or, alternatively, Mad, Sad and Glad.

In an environment that fully embraces retrospectives, any member of the team can propose a retrospective at any time.

An Invitation to Take Action

Would you and your team like to be deliberately developmental? For many, it's easy to answer "yes" to this question. It is more challenging to maintain an ongoing intention and consistently do the work required to bring the philosophy to life. Keep this challenge in mind as we move into Chapter 10 where we explore the concept of rituals and routines. How might you go about embedding a deliberately developmental mindset into the fiber of your organization using routines?

To be a DDO, effective feedback is a must. The best way to improve feedback is through practice. Push through the inevitable emotional reluctance and take action. To get started, try a few of the following ideas.

- Identify the feedback approach that feels best to you and make a point of using it consistently within the next week.
- Seek out feedback from someone you trust and observe the approach they use.
- Give permission for others to be more candid and direct with you.
- Coach someone else to provide feedback rather than allowing yourself to become an intermediary.

Chapter 10

SUSTAINING WHAT MATTERS

ROUTINES AND RITUALS

The SideFX software development team has a doughnut table. It's round and sits in the center of the development floor. From time to time someone will bring boxes of doughnuts, enough to feed the whole department. When do the doughnuts arrive? The day after the nightly software build breaks. If a developer has committed code that breaks the nightly software compile, he or she is responsible for bringing doughnuts the next morning.

Over the years, the bringing of doughnuts has become a fun and meaningful ritual. It sends the message that messing with live code is a big deal; that smart people make mistakes; and that learning is an ongoing process worth celebrating.

Rituals are the tools of purposeful habit building. By doing something intentionally on a routine basis, we build muscle memory. We also reinforce what is most important to us. Things

SideFX Doughnut Rules

"Any who breaks the build shall deliver unto R&D two dozen doughnuts.

If thou hath broke the build yesterday and on the morrow have not fixed the build, thou shalt deliver unto R&D *three* dozen doughnuts.

Each sunrise thenceforth which finds the build still broken shall double the tariff due R&D.

Upon the fifth day, doughnuts shall no longer appease R&D; those who hath sundered the build must appear with cake, or not at all.

Whomsoever doth eat the last doughnut shall, in recompense, discard the box forthwith. Don't just leave it there. That's dirty behavior and if we catch you doing it, you will be buying... ANOTHER BOX OF DOUGHNUTS!

Lust not after doughnuts with holes in, for they are the devil's work, and an abomination."

– SideFX Internal Wiki

that may initially feel unnatural and awkward become habitual and even comfortable.

We have each experienced the power of habit. If we get up at the same time each morning, brush our teeth, meditate or do some free writing, exercise and drink a smoothie, those individual activities become habits forming our healthy morning routine. We can just as easily fall into an unhealthy morning routine of sleeping in, skipping the gym and grabbing a quick pastry.

Organizations can also build unhealthy habits which, once in place, are hard to break. Alternatively, rituals create healthy habits to sustain successful company cultures.

Rituals, and the resulting habits, are anchor points of social connection. Many rituals are anchored in food—regular team lunches, celebratory meals or sharing homemade baking. These events bring people together and break down social hierarchies.

Steven Handel, author at *The Emotion Machine,* suggests the following as characteristics of rituals. Rituals...

> ...are symbolic and meaningful.
> ...are internally motivated.
> ...require full engagement.
> ...are anchored in celebration.
> ...tell a story.
> ...bring a sense of belonging.
> ...focus on the performance of tasks.

Rituals range from traditional and practical to unique and crazy. They often begin when a one-time action, story or phrase is embraced and repeated by the team. Other times, significant planning goes into developing a ritual and associated cadence.

One ritual, which may seem silly but helps participants leave video meetings with a smile is having an "I'm out" action. The Enspiral Foundation Catalyst team ends meetings with attendees making a "victory arms" gesture, while the Golden Pandas team makes panda ears. In contrast, the morning stand-up (described later in this chapter) is a prime example of a more traditional and practical ritual.

In organizations where colleagues are autonomous and self-select how and with whom to work, being explicit about routines and rituals takes on a heightened level of importance.

Cadence

Cadence is the flow or rhythm of events. It's like the pulse of the organization, bringing predictability to an otherwise chaotic environment. Cadence creates a regular schedule for showing work and delivering value.

Agile processes work in two-week iterations or sprints. In contrast, bulkier multi-stage projects traditionally have highly variable milestones with little sense of cadence.

Let's look at a few examples of how cadence plays a key role in various teams' rituals.

The entire Percolab team meets for two hours every Tuesday at 10 am; their meetings are open to anybody, including the public. The check-in, agenda building, approach to decision-making and checkout are all rituals within their weekly meeting routine.

The Enspiral Foundation Catalysts use a two-week rhythm of Scrum sprints to manage their work and communicate progress to the network. The predictable heartbeat and consistent flow of the sprints allows individuals to jump in and out of work commitments according to their availability and energy. In addition, the partially distributed team at Enspiral comes together in its entirety for a retreat twice a year to provide an opportunity for deeper connection. Within the retreats are rituals, like story circles, Open Space and shared meals.

Percolab Guests

Percolab routinely invites guests to attend their weekly team meetings.

"Some of the guests at meetings are interested in collaborating with us, some want to study us for academic purposes, some attend our meetings so they can learn about self-management and maybe even bring new practices to their own organizations, some are international experts passing through Montreal who want to jam with us, some are clients we already work with, others are thinking of working with us for the first time— attending our meetings gives them a really good practical sense of our applied knowledge. One of my favorite things to do is invite all the participants in my workshops to come to a team meeting. You should see their faces!"

– Elizabeth Hunt, Percolab

Some rituals are tied to a triggering event or a milestone, such as the SideFX team's sharing of doughnuts when the software goes down. Similarly, many teams schedule celebrations when major objectives are achieved.

S3, a business methodology we explore in Chapter 14, advises that reviews of decisions and agreements be scheduled no further than six months apart as a ritualized way of maintaining clarity and relevance. This ensures the team doesn't fall into the trap of ignoring something just because it's not flagged as an issue.

Simple and Powerful Rituals

Two of the most common, easiest and powerful rituals are meeting **check-ins** and **check-outs**. The idea is simple.

When you are with a new group, a check-in welcomes everyone into the space and provides an opportunity for important things to be said. This is usually completed by going around the physical or virtual room and having each individual speak what's top of mind. Responses may include, "I'm looking forward to this meeting," or "I'm not sure why I'm at this meeting," or "I just had a frustrating call and I'm distracted."

The ritual of speaking your state of mind is important not only to the speaker but also to others in the space. It gives everyone a clue as to where people are at and opens the possibility for more trust and honesty. While people sometimes say what they think the group wants or needs to hear, over time, this practice creates an environment where everyone feels comfortable being authentic.

Questions are often asked in check-in circles which can be used to both lighten the mood and allow you to get to know the other attendees better. Social media tool provider Buffer[1] and collaboration specialist Amanda Fenton[2] have both published great check-in questions. Here are a few examples:

- What's the best thing that happened to you today?
- What are you most excited about right now?
- What's the last picture you took on your phone?
- What habit or improvement are you working on?
- What problem do you wish you could solve?
- What's one new and interesting thing you've been thinking about lately?

- What is your personal weather status (cloudy, foggy, sunny, etc.)?
- What's one thing you're really proud of that you'd like to share with the group?
- Why did you accept the invitation to join this gathering?
- What are you seeking to learn and contribute?

Check-outs are similar and provide a way to close with a quick parting thought. A frequently used check-out question is, "What's one word to describe how you are leaving this meeting?"

The Daily Standup is another ritual from the agile community. It's a meeting that happens every day in the same place at the same time. As a quick connection point, it allows everyone on the team to understand what's happening day-to-day. Four elements define the daily standup:

1. Everyone stands.
2. Everyone participates, whether attending in person or virtually.
3. It's NOT a dialogue, problem-solving session or forum for lengthy information sharing.
4. One person at a time answers these three questions:
   a. What did you do yesterday?
   b. What are you going to do today?
   c. What are the impediments that could prevent you from delivering?

When done well, standups take 15 to 20 minutes regardless of the group size. Standing reminds everyone not to get too comfortable or talk too long.

Retreats

Rituals are often attached to events, such as retreats. Retreats are not the same as off-site meetings although they may include similar elements. These events might focus on a particular topic, or may be checkpoints in your organization's ongoing journey. Retreats tend to offer extra time and space for colleagues to be together, relax, play and relate away from the confines of normal routine.

Depending on the group and intention of the gathering, retreats can be anything from camping trips to catered stays at purpose-built venues. The key is to have the group stay together for an uninterrupted, extended period of time.

Szabolcs Emich, an agile coach and facilitator from Hungary, believes in this idea so much that his consulting practice sells three-month residential innovation retreats to multi-national companies. His results show that all measures of happiness and performance rise when teammates work and live together. We aren't suggesting this level of intensity or time commitment is possible or necessary for everyone, merely that extended retreats are an option worth consideration.

Greaterthan is an organization whose products and services allow companies and teams to collectively budget and spend money. As a globally distributed team of digital nomads, Greaterthan has ritualized a pattern of seven- to ten-day, in-person work sprints four to six times per year. The six-person team temporarily lives and works together in amazing locations to become invigorated by collective focus and flow. They assert that the recharge from these intense collaborations easily gets them through the next quarter of working solo from different timezones.

As you plan your first retreats, rituals may need to be defined through agreement-making. Will attendance for sessions be optional or mandatory? Will there be alcohol at your retreat? Are laptops and smartphones permitted?

Over time these agreements become part of the rhythm. At Enspiral, for example, there is an agreement that story circles happen with no alcohol or substance use before or during this ritual. This act of sanctifying the space offers a level of safety that those substances can sometimes interrupt.

Finding Opportunities to Experiment

Humans are creatures of habit. When left to chance, we stumble into both good and bad routines. Our invitation is for you to become more intentional in the habits you and your colleagues create together.

Small, simple rituals can have a significant reinforcing effect on individual and team behaviors. Some rituals may come out of an intentional team or organization social contract such as, "We'll have lunch together every Thursday," or "We will all block Monday mornings for a team planning session." Other rituals drift into playful or whimsical territory: "If you're at work on your birthday, you will be invited to spend the day wearing an adult-sized banana onesie."

In closing this chapter, our invitation is to notice your organization's cultural patterns. What rituals and routines already exist, even if unnamed? Which ones are important enough to name, emphasize and proactively support? Perhaps you'll even notice some patterns you want to let go. Allow space for a range of ideas, including fun and silly ones, to take on a life of their own.

Chapter 11

THE TABOO TOPIC OF COMPENSATION

A FRESH PERSPECTIVE ON VALUE EXCHANGE

Tales of organizations making salaries transparent abound, and rightfully so. Discovering what your colleague earns compared to you can bring up all sorts of emotions. It's no surprise that transparent compensation is often fodder for gossip and judgement. Is it equitable pay for equitable work? How is equitable work measured? Are the measures objective and fair?

Compensation traditionally consists of three pillars: salary, bonus and equity.

Salaries intend to fairly value an individual's day-to-day contributions. The process of setting salaries usually gravitates to regimented, inflexible formulas or is hidden to avoid revealing discrepancies and prompting difficult conversations.

Bonuses are most often used as part of a carrot-and-stick approach to influencing performance. They also mitigate the risk of expenses outpacing revenues.

Ownership and equity aim to reward risk-taking, build a sense of personal connection and retain team members.

Although logical in theory, you may sense how these three compensation pillars feel out of step with many of the concepts we've been exploring in *Reinventing Scale-Ups*. The traditional approach to compensation is deeply rooted in putting human resources into boxes to be measured and priced.

> In his popular online video, business and behavior expert Dan Pink debunks the myth that bonuses motivate better performance.[1] He explains why traditional bonus schemes can often impair performance. **Science shows that roles requiring even rudimentary cognitive skill benefit more from a focus on autonomy, mastery and purpose than on financial reward.** Despite this knowledge, compensation based on production numbers, sales, customer feedback and other KPI's abound.

In self-managed organizations, setting compensation tends to rely much more on transparency, crowd-sourced data and negotiation. Many progressive organizations have removed bonus plans altogether, choosing instead to use company-wide profit sharing. Company ownership becomes rebalanced to better represent both individual contributions and risk, with greater fairness applied in determining how the pie gets sliced.

You and your team will need to create a compensation system that works best for your organization. Our goal here is to share examples of compensation approaches which challenge the status quo.

Morning Star – Self-Set Salaries

Morning Star, the world's leading tomato-ingredient processing company, is seen as a trailblazer in many areas of self-management. The company uses a self-set salary process in which each team of colleagues is advised on the total percentage of pay adjustment available. It's up to each individual to make their own decision on what personal adjustment they believe appropriate. They then justify their decision, send it to a number of colleagues for feedback, and advocate for their final number.

The Moment – Capability Mapping

The Moment is a ten-person and growing consulting firm led by three founders. The team is internally transparent with compensation and embraces many other progressive philosophies. As the team expanded, a project was launched to design a scalable compensation approach. The team developed a comprehensive competency rubric consisting of 26 different measures that allowed each team member to plot their personal development, both as a consultant and a contributor to the business. Individuals then completed a self-assessment against the 26 measures and asked three colleagues, including one founder, for input. The four colleagues then met, shared reflections and discussed the ratings. At his or her own discretion, the individual then updated their self-assessment based on the feedback received. The final ratings mapped to a compensation matrix. All final self-ratings were made visible to the entire team.

In this first attempt at developing an open compensation framework, the process turned out to be beneficial, but not for the reasons intended. The founders were uncomfortable with the final ratings, realizing team members had differing interpretations of the rubric. Rather than using the data directly, the founders made final compensation decisions with the data as a significant input. They were transparent with the team every step of the journey and sought advice regularly. In the end, the team had the opportunity to travel the compensation journey with the founders, gain meaningful feedback from colleagues, strengthen their working relationships and feel even greater ownership for the business.

Going forward, the team is committed to building on their learning and refining the process. They are now exploring software solutions to help remove personal bias from self-assessments. In reflection, co-founder Greg Judelman says, "Designing a scalable compensation approach has taken us more time than anticipated and required personal courage by everyone involved. But it's been worth it—we've grown and gelled as a team and have a clear sense of the collective values that we're working and living for."

Fitzii – Collaborative Salary Setting

All employees at Fitzii know each other's salaries, and detailed company financials are available for review each month. After their first year, each team member is eligible to participate in the annual Salary Advice Process, where they seek the advice of their peers, investigate the market and understand how their compensation fits within the budget. Equipped with that information, individuals decide on their salary and publish their reasoning. Interestingly, team members routinely pay themselves less (not more) than they would have had they had bosses.

Buffer – Fully Transparent Compensation

Buffer published an instructive article on how they calculate team salaries.[2] They factor in market data, location, cost of living, role value, experience, loyalty and risk tolerance. This system makes salary calculations fair and transparent. It also provides team members direct visibility on how they can increase their compensation. Buffer publishes everyone's salary publicly on their website.

Enspiral – Needs-based Compensation

At Enspiral, small teams known as livelihood pods have open conversations about personal needs. Based on the concept of abundance, everyone requests and receives the minimum they need to sustain themselves. Two examples of livelihood pods are Root Systems[3] (software developers) and Golden Pandas[4] (facilitators, consultants and teachers). As revenues generated by the livelihood pods increase, compensation conversations follow.

The Root Systems livelihood pod uses the following formula for calculating a month's pay:

Base Income + Business Viability Bonus + Performance Bonus

- Base Income is the monthly amount a core member will always receive, no matter how many hours they work.
- The Business Viability Bonus is an additional amount paid based on how sustainable the team perceives the business to be.
- A Performance Bonus is added based on work that brings money to the organization.

How exactly these different amounts are calculated depends on the team's current financial buffer and the activity types conducted during the month.

HolacracyOne – Crowd-sourced Compensation

HolacracyOne is the consulting and training company behind Holacracy, which we explore further in Chapter 14. At HolacracyOne, co-workers fill out a survey for all their colleagues, consisting of only two ratings: (i) This person contributes (much) more or (much) less than me (on a scale from +3 to -3); and (ii) This person has a good basis to evaluate me (on a scale of 1 to 5). An algorithm is used to process the data collected and colleagues are grouped into salary buckets. As a result, "The more experienced, knowledgeable and hard-working people land in the higher buckets that earn bigger salaries; the more junior, less experienced colleagues naturally gravitate toward buckets with lower salaries."[5]

Valve – Centralized Compensation Team

The team at software company Valve takes a more centralized approach to compensation. A designated group of employees (which changes over time) interviews everyone in the company annually. They ask for feedback on each individual the interviewee has worked with over the past year. The information collected is used primarily for constructive feedback. They also ask the individual to rank each member of his or her own project or product group on four metrics: (1) Skill Level/Technical Ability, (2) Productivity/Output, (3) Group Contribution and (4) Product Contribution. Each of these metrics is given equal weight in compiling a stack ranking of all employees and is used to determine compensation.

Miovision – Compensation Sponsorship

Each member of the Miovision team has someone who sponsors their compensation. It's up to the compensation sponsors throughout the organization to ensure team members are paid fairly. When compensation issues arise, the sponsor works through the issue with a shared responsibility to the company and the individual.

A Few Words on Ownership

When a team is comprised of the right people who communicate openly, make commitments to one another, and support each other's growth, there is the possibility of a different sort of relationship to risk and ownership. If a founder believes in the importance and value of nurturing a creative spirit and energy—their own and others—their philosophies on ownership can play an important role. We can't ignore or discount the emotional labor most founders endure when building an organization—and the feeling of responsibility and accountability they have for the livelihood of their colleagues. Collectively reconciling our relationship to money and ownership can be the single most important action we take to freeing up creativity and entrepreneurship in our organizations.

Entrepreneur, author and lecturer Mike Moyer has written extensively about a philosophy for fairly distributing equity. *Slicing Pie* is "a simple formula based on the principle that a person's percent share of the equity should always be equal to that person's share of the at-risk contributions. At-risk contributions include time, money, ideas, relationships, supplies, equipment, facilities or anything else someone provides without full payment of its fair market value."[6]

This means anyone who risks more, such as a founder whose salary goes unpaid early on, would be compensated over time with a greater share of the profit. This approach provides ways to accommodate colleagues with differing risk profiles. It also allows people to evolve their equity agreements when their risk profiles shift due to other life changes.

Beyond Compensation

The philosophies in this chapter can be applied to external relationships, too. Knowing that transparency breeds trust,

Buffer shares its pricing model online.[7] Customers know exactly where their money goes.

Some workshop providers transparently share costs with participants. In this case, a workshop fee is published up front but it's not until after the event that all revenues and expenses are finalized. Any shortfall gets divided by the number of participants and each participant chooses whether or not to pay their share of the outstanding balance.

There are endless ways to start experimenting with broadening financial transparency in your value exchanges with customers, suppliers and other stakeholders. Where might you try out some different approaches?

Getting Started

Discussing compensation is challenging, even in teams where psychological safety has been well established. If you are ready to start exploring new and different compensation approaches, here are some suggestions for the journey.

- Invite input from all those impacted.
- Make sure to get expert input around compliance and legal issues.
- Be clear on who the decision-maker is for any change.
- Be transparent about the decision-making process and provide updates each step of the way.
- Establish guiding principles for compensation design.
- Provide ample time for the process to unfold without undue pressure.
- Tune into how easily old compensation paradigms can influence thinking.
- Consider using a third-party facilitator to help guide the process.

Chapter 12

CHOOSING FUTURE COLLEAGUES

INVITING (RECRUITING) TEAM MEMBERS

Are reinvented, self-managed, agile organizations for everyone? The simple answer is "No." Self-organizing companies tend to operate with considerable ambiguity. For some, that ambiguity can be too challenging, and feel unsafe. Most of these companies involve the entire team in choosing their new colleagues, providing everyone with an opportunity to explore fit prior to committing. By creating transparency into your unique environment and spreading the word widely, those who find themselves drawn to this new way of working will seek you out.

In his book, *It's Not the How or the What but the Who: Succeed by Surrounding Yourself with the Best*, Claudio Fernández-Aráoz shares five indicators for exploring an individual's potential. Although not specifically focused on self-managed companies, this list of attributes prepares individuals for the increased independence required to operate in these environments.

Motivation – Having the ambition to excel in the pursuit of unselfish, collective goals. Showing deep personal humility and a focus on self-improvement.

Curiosity – Looking for new experiences, knowledge and feedback. Open to learning and change.

Insight – Ability to gather and make sense of information that suggests new possibilities.

Engagement – Capacity to use emotion and logic to communicate a persuasive vision and connect with people.

Determination – Ability to fight for difficult goals despite challenges.

In his article, "12 Keys to the Workplace of the Future," Doug Kirkpatrick adds that the most important indicators for an individual to fit into a self-managed environment are **grit** and **initiative**.[1]

As with compensation, team-based self-reflection and experimentation will help you identify the most appropriate indicators for fit with your organization. For inspiration, we've collected various recruiting practices from reinvented scale-ups.

Percolab – Trial Collaboration

The team at Percolab places high value on sharing experiences with potential candidates in advance of any hiring decisions. It usually begins when a candidate attends Percolab's weekly meeting, which is open to the public. Since Percolab's tactical meeting style is unique compared to most organizations, a guest immediately experiences how team members relate to one another and what they value as a group. If it feels like a fit, both parties might seek to collaborate on a project. No promises or commitments are made beyond seeing how collaboration feels and works. If the first project works out well, and if the individual desires a more formal and committed relationship, they are invited to write a letter to the team expressing their intentions.

Thereafter, in an online space (Loomio) each person in the team shares their honest thoughts and feelings about the idea of this new person joining. Once everyone has spoken, a decision is made to bring the person in or not. If there are no objections, a contract is prepared. It is the candidate who chooses three people from the team to sign the contract. The signatories clarify the final details, such as transitioning out of current commitments or working around planned travel. Once completed, the employee gets full access to the online conversation about their potential hiring. This establishes a transparent culture and puts the developmental process into motion.

The Percolab process is rooted in an understanding of the accountabilities and expectations of working in a self-managed organization. It requires a level of grit and initiative on the part of anyone interested in joining the team.

It's provocative to flip the recruitment process on its head by having prospects lead the interaction. Could we imagine a time when recruiting moves beyond the current model, making acceptance or rejection more equal between parties?

Menlo Innovations – Group Recruiting

Menlo Innovations is a 45-person software-development and consulting firm focused on maximizing quality and project agility through the use of integrated project teams. Menlo hires via large group auditions without having the interviewers look at resumes in advance. Interviewees are paired together during three twenty-minute exercises to evaluate culture fit. Those that pass this initial audition are invited back for a full day interview.

All software development and user experience design work at Menlo is done in pairs, so the full day "interview" is spent doing paired projects and coding or designing with other Menlo employees.

Menlo is looking for "good kindergarten skills"—the ability to learn, grow and play together. Unlike most tech companies, Menlo isn't trying to hire for specific technical skills. They believe software development requires constant learning.

Following the interview day, the team makes a collective decision on who they'd like to consider further. Those individuals are then invited back for three weeks of paid work. If the team feels their initial assessment still holds, the relationship is extended to full-time employment.

With Menlo's paired approach, the team is able to assess a large volume of candidates in a single day by pairing each candidate with a current team member. Using this approach, they can double the size of their team within weeks if needed. Anyone selected to join Menlo has already had a meaningful team experience and started building personal relationships.

With no one looking at resumes before the interview, diversity at Menlo is greater than most other tech companies. Their team includes people with degrees in philosophy, astronomy, physics and early-childhood education—and that's the norm, not the exception. Menlo's experimental approach has proven that removing traditional resume bias helps increase the diversity of candidates who will thrive within an organization.

Wellbeing Teams – Values-based Recruitment

Wellbeing Teams are small, self-managing, neighborhood-based groups supporting people to live well at home in their communities. Tasks and challenges are used in values-based recruitment processes to identify and retain team members who have the values, attitudes and aspirations necessary for work in health and care.[2] Examples of values and associated recruiting processes include:

Self-management – Individuals who can work effectively in a team without traditional management structures. Recruiting tasks for drawing out aligned values include:

- Asking candidates to participate with the interviewer in giving each other feedback to demonstrate their skill and approach.
- "Reverse interviews" where representatives of the organization are interviewed about the role by candidates to demonstrate their curiosity in seeking out valuable information.
- Asking candidates to contribute to the recruitment day, for example by bringing food and participating in a shared lunch. This is an opportunity to explore the individual's approach to sharing and teamwork.

Authenticity – Care and support roles benefit from people bringing their "whole self" to work, rather than coming with a sanitized "work persona." Exercises include:

- Starting the recruiting process by crafting a "Could this be you?" role description that goes far beyond qualifications and experience, inviting the individual to bring more of their life experience into the process.
- Sharing with the candidate one-page "whole self" personal profiles of everyone involved in the recruiting process.
- Introducing a human bingo game at the beginning of the process that invites candidates to learn personal and professional information about the interviewers and others they meet along the way.

A person-centred outlook – People whose values are rooted in care and compassion, and have the ability to express and demonstrate these values in their work. Opportunities to identify these values include:

- Creating situations where candidates are called upon to identify what really matters to others in the room.
- Demonstrating physicality, comfort and readiness to engage with others through hand massage.

LeadWise – Dating

LeadWise is a digital learning platform and community guided by the philosophies of organizational changemaker Ricardo Semler. Ian Borges from LeadWise describes their recruitment process as dating: "Before getting into serious relationships, people generally date in order to get to know and see if they actually like each other."[3] When facing the serious decision of finding a life partner, we escalate our commitment over a period of time. LeadWise uses the same approach to expanding its team.

The LeadWise process involves five steps:

1. Full transparency

From the start, LeadWise is open with its recruitment process. It starts by setting up a video call with the candidate. All team members are invited to join this exploratory chat. Following the call, the candidate may be invited onto the team's basic platforms and communication tools. With this invitation, the candidate has access to all company information including financial projections, team salaries and strategy documents.

2. Autonomous exploration

With self-organization and autonomy as LeadWise's core values, the LeadWise team expects a proactive posture and doesn't micromanage the candidate. It's a good test to check the candidate's ability to self-manage. At this point some candidates don't connect and organically disengage, bringing a natural end to the recruitment dating process.

3. Short assignment

LeadWise invites candidates to start collaborating on a short assignment as a way to experience the candidate's level of engagement, see specific skills in action and begin building personal connections. The assignment can be part of an ongoing or new project. Depending on its length and complexity, the assignment may be paid or unpaid. Examples of assignments include building a landing page, editing a video, managing a community for a month, co-designing a course structure, writing a few pieces of content or designing an e-book.

4. Reality check

After delivering the assignment or spending enough time to get the feeling of working together, another video call is organized. It's here that both LeadWise and the candidate get to share first impressions and feedback. Team members are invited to join the discussions and a recording of the call is available for all.

5. Compensation agreement

If all stakeholders are satisfied and confident after this first experience, the candidate suggests their own compensation proposal. If the proposal is fair and LeadWise is able to fund it, agreements are set. Most team members work as freelancers with great autonomy, taking on other projects as they wish.

Based on this process, LeadWise has experienced the following benefits:

- A more transparent and trustful process.
- Minimized surprises and disappointments in both directions.
- An easier path to identifying values and culture fit.

- Greater insights and concrete experiences to sustain the final compensation agreement.
- A more friendly and informal process.
- Ease in building a sustainable relationship from the beginning.

Enspiral – Create Your Own Job

At Enspiral, where most of the structural work is done on a voluntary basis, the core challenge to finding new collaborators is time, not money. Since Enspiral doesn't employ anybody, it's up to the individual to negotiate a way in and find their place. Where can they do their best work and make their best contribution? In this way, the very idea of recruitment doesn't exist. It's all on the potential contributor to navigate, propose and ultimately decide.

Putting it into Practice

It is difficult during an interview process, or an initiation period, to really know if the fit of the new person is right for both them and the team. Many organizations have long relied on the concept of a three-month-trial period, which can be expensive. It's also dependent on the quality of the onboarding process and what metrics are being assessed.

Only you and your team can decide what is best for recruiting new members into your organization. Our invitation is for you to look at recruiting through a broader lens. Many traditional recruiting processes seem mechanical, almost unhuman. Get curious about your process and seek feedback from recent new hires. What are the routines and rituals you use now? What do they tell candidates about your values as a company? How will you invite candidates to interact with your company? How can you meaningfully test for fit and allow candidates to do the same? Recruiting will be a never-ending journey of discovery, with each new role and candidate offering an opportunity to experiment.

Turning Recruitment on It's Head

"What if we imagine a world of work where potential employees exercise their agency in identifying opportunities and proposing relationships? It becomes an opportunity and a challenge for the person seeking a different environment in which to earn their livelihood. They need to put in the requisite work to understand where and with whom they choose to do that work. It's a big leap in the traditional sense of recruiting but a reality for many freelancers. Websites like Glassdoor provide reviews of companies by employees, putting the power of information into the hands of job seekers. Like any rating system, it's flawed and subjective, but as far as I can tell it's also open and transparent. Fairygodboss.com is another workplace review site to help women understand how various companies perform from a gender diversity perspective."

– Susan

Chapter 13

THE NEW JOINER EXPERIENCE

ONBOARDING NEW TEAM MEMBERS

Onboarding is a frequently missed opportunity. There's no better way to unintentionally say "We don't really care about you" than through a minimal investment in welcoming new team members. On the flip side, an awesome onboarding experience pays dividends to everyone involved. Joiners are more likely to stay, team performance will be higher and relationships are built more quickly and with intention.

How you choose to recruit individuals onto the team will influence how you shape onboarding. If you embrace the "trial period" approach, recruiting and onboarding become intertwined. If, instead, your recruitment process leans toward a more traditional flow, onboarding is seen as its own distinct phase. The content of this chapter applies to both scenarios and is written with the two-phase recruiting-followed-by-onboarding approach in mind.

What is (Awesome) Onboarding?

Onboarding is a tactical list of tasks and experiences giving newcomers what they need to get started. When done well, individuals understand expectations, company culture, the various elements of their work and how things actually get done day-to-day. It's a celebration.

Transitioning into a new company is rife with uncertainty. Did I make the right decision? Do I like these people? Do they like me? Am I competent in this role? Am I seen as worthy?

How will you know if you've delivered an awesome onboarding process? Proactively setting the bar high is key. Compare these two examples:

> *Our onboarding process ensures every new team member has the supplies they need, understands the job and integrates into the team by the end of their first week.*

> *Versus...*

> *By the end of our onboarding process, every new joiner believes there is no better place to work. They are fully participating, contributing and meeting commitments. They feel like they've found their tribe.*

Can you feel the difference?

Traditionally we think of onboarding as an "integration." How fast can we integrate the newbie into our team? How fast can we get this person to think and work like us? A more powerful approach is to ask, "How fast can we create an environment for new team members to be fully contributing as *themselves*?" The willingness of everyone to share fears, weaknesses and uncertainties removes mental distractions. Space for personal and team development gets created faster.

Goal of onboarding – How fast can we create an environment for new team members to be fully contributing as themselves?

The Pre-onboarding Phase

Onboarding is often viewed as a one-day or one-week event beginning when the joiner shows up for the first time. It's true the first few days are critically important, but there is so much more.

The process begins with the first interaction a candidate has with your company. Most times it's reading a published document, such as your website, or having an introductory conversation. In those early moments, impressions are created. Mental images start forming. The new joiner will use these newly set expectations to evaluate their first week at your company. Exceed those expectations and all is good.

Unfortunately, we often unintentionally oversell what we can deliver. Within days of joining, things start going sideways and disappointments start mounting. With attention and planning, new joiners will exit their onboarding phase feeling fully valued and pleased with their decision to become part of your team.

Meetings and conversations with candidates are a goldmine of information in helping shape an awesome onboarding experience. By paying attention to what the individual enjoys and values, you have an opportunity to incorporate these passions into the process. For example, if your new team member is a soccer fanatic, consider scheduling a lunch with someone on the team who shares their passion. Each team within the company has the ability to create unique experiences in bonding with their new peer.

The window of time between when the individual commits to joining and actually joins the team is fertile with opportunities for positive interactions. Send a welcome package to the joiner and their family. Have their team members reach out by phone or schedule coffee. Write a personal note. A few simple actions will go along way in over-delivering on expectations.

Three Essential Onboarding Tools

1. Role Description

It's important new joiners understand what success looks like. Percolab's role format, as shared in Chapter 6, offers a template. Sharing and shaping this document with the new joiner during the recruiting and onboarding phases ensures ongoing alignment.

2. Checklist

An onboarding checklist is an essential tool. That, in itself, is not rocket science. Here's the key: experiment with creating one comprehensive master onboarding checklist covering every new joiner. The process starts by creating a list for a specific individual. For subsequent hires, use the same list and add anything new. On the checklist, include a timeframe column for each task. Use a label, such as "Not Required" for items that were critical for previous new joiners but not for this individual. Repeat this process every time you onboard someone new. In no time, you will have a single onboarding checklist that can be customized in minutes. As an added bonus, each new joiner gains an appreciation for the different things other team members have needed to learn.

In preparing checklist content, consider incorporating four distinct components:

1. **Education** – How can the individual learn the things needed to quickly become a wildly successful contributor?
2. **Observation** – How can the individual benefit by observing others? Many people learn best by watching others in action.
3. **Activation** – What, exactly, does the individual need to do, experience or complete to build their own competence and confidence?
4. **Demonstration** – What does the team need to see the individual demonstrate as part of the process of building trust in their new colleague's capabilities?

To bring the checklist concept to life, consider the example of a new joiner entering a sales role.

- Education: They will first need to learn about the products and services they will be selling by reading company documents, reviewing previous sales presentations and asking questions of their colleagues.
- Observation: As a next step, they are likely to shadow one or more colleagues in a few prospect meetings.
- Activation: Before leading their first prospect meeting, they may choose to complete several role plays.
- Demonstration: Lastly, they will likely be joined in their first sales calls by a colleague who will observe and provide coaching. Once the colleague is comfortable, the new joiner will be ready to move forward on their own.

You can create the checklist in a spreadsheet or document file. Using a tool such as Trello or Asana helps create transparency and simplifies updating and versioning.

3. Buddies

Many companies assign a buddy as someone to help new joiners during their first few weeks. Unfortunately, this role often doesn't get the attention it deserves. In organizations using self-management principles, the buddy role becomes critical.

The team at Fitzii assigns a "sponsor" for each new hire. That person is 100 percent responsible for the success and engagement of their new joiner.

Rather than assigning a single buddy, Buffer uses a trilogy: a leader buddy, a role buddy and a culture buddy.

> *The Leader Buddy is a very experienced member of the team who has practiced and experienced having tough conversations around helping [new joiners] live to the Buffer values.*

> *The Role Buddy is someone on the team who understands the role which the [new joiner] is joining the team to play.*

> *The Culture Buddy is an experienced member of the team who has shown that they consistently are able to give great praise around the culture-fit of new and existing team members.*

Who Owns Onboarding?

Once you have a solid checklist and buddy process, it's time to get to work. But who owns the onboarding process in a self-managing company? We advocate having the joiner take charge of the process with the support of buddies. No one cares more about the joiner's onboarding than him or herself. Hand the checklist to the joiner on day one and clarify that the ultimate responsibility falls to them. Use the buddy as an accountability partner and someone who can raise a red flag if the process starts slipping.

Onboarding Ideas

Developing a solid and effective onboarding process is a minimal requirement. An absolutely knock-it-out-of-the-park process separates the top performing companies from the rest. Here are a few examples to prime your thinking as you consider the best approach for your unique circumstances.

- **Make the first impression memorable**
  - Plan a team-wide or company-wide fun event to end the first week. Ensure it's something your new joiner will love based on your knowledge of their passions. If you're hiring fast, group new joiners together in cohorts so you can appropriately celebrate without being overwhelmed.
  - Cloud computing company Rackspace populates its onboarding effort with "games, skits, costumes, thumping music and a limbo bar."[1] What could be more memorable than that?
- **Share company history**
  - Ray Cao, the CEO of marketing services company Exact Media, wrote a letter to all team members sharing his personal history and experiences from the early days of building the company. All joiners receive that letter in their first week. A one-on-one chat with Ray follows shortly thereafter to talk about the history of the company in more detail.
  - Tech firm Bazaarvoice sends incoming employees on a week-long scavenger hunt designed to bring them up to speed on company culture and company jargon.

- **Build in cultural rituals**
  - Moving and storage company Guardian Removals takes joiners for a walk around the local area ending at a cafe they've been visiting for years. For fun, the joiner then gets creative ordering food and drinks for everyone.
  - TINYpulse, a Seattle-based employee engagement software provider, tasks joiners with purchasing an object they believe represents the company's values. During the company's biweekly team meeting, they present the object and share why they picked it.
- **Invest in learning the core business**
  - Exceptional customer service is core to accounting software company FreshBooks' business. The company is an example of how prioritizing values in the onboarding process takes commitment. Every new member of the FreshBooks team spends a full month working in customer support before jumping into their actual role. The company is unwavering in this element of the onboarding process. The result is an award-winning customer service orientation that permeates every part of the company.
  - At FAVI, a company specializing in pressure die casting, newly hired engineers and administrative team members are trained at operating at least one machine on the shop floor.
- **Purposefully build relationships**
  - The first thing anyone joining Fitzii, or their parent company the Ian Martin Group, does on their first day is to go desk-to-desk with their sponsor, delivering tasty treats and taking selfies with their new friends that are then published on the internal messaging system.

- Every new contributor at Enspiral has a steward—someone they can rely on to help navigate the network. In addition, there are cohorts of new contributors who work on projects for a three-month period. In this way, there are bonds formed between new contributors and across the broader network.

- **Closing out the onboarding process**
  - At the end of green-energy-provider Bullfrog Power's 12-week onboarding process, new joiners have a wrap-up meeting with the onboarding process owner to share learnings and help improve the experience for the future.
  - At FAVI, joiners end their onboarding process by writing a free-format open letter to their group of colleagues sharing thoughts about their experience and gratitude to those who helped them along the way.

How would you rate the effectiveness of your onboarding process on a scale of zero to ten? How do your recent joiners rate it? If it's not a solid and consistent eight, nine or ten, consider investing some time in stepping up the awesomeness by a notch or two. Experiment with a few additions to the process. Invite the team to get creative. Learn from each onboarding to improve the next. Before long, your investment will begin paying dividends.

Chapter 14

MOVING BEYOND TRADITIONAL HIERARCHIES

BRINGING STRUCTURE TO TEAMS

Throughout the book, we've shared philosophies and tools based on an agile, ecosystemic approach to organizing. Each philosophy and tool is powerful on its own and offers new ways for leaders and colleagues to experiment. We've left the most significant and deeply rooted element of traditional business for last. Despite the effectiveness of everything we've shared so far, real change may be elusive if your organization is structured as a hierarchy. Structure implicitly influences all areas of business, even when it's impact isn't readily apparent.

Although there are compelling reasons to abandon hierarchical structures, scale-ups usually start pyramid-building early. Most business books, academics and software platforms continue to focus on top-down organizing principles. There are other options. New structures and associated software tools exist to redefine workplace relationships.

The following four approaches outline new and different ways of operating.

Holacracy by HolacracyOne

Holacracy is an operating system borne out of the experiences of Brian Robertson. Brian founded Ternary Software in 2001. The startup software company became a laboratory for experiments designed to answer the question, "What gets in the way of people working together as effectively and efficiently as possible?" Brian partnered with entrepreneur Tom Thomison to take what he'd learned and develop it into an operating system. As it evolved through trial and error, the system became known as Holacracy.

Holacracy is a rigid set of principles and rules intended to be adopted by an organization with little initial customization. On the company's website, Holacracy is described as bringing "structure and discipline to a peer-to-peer workplace." It's designed to offer an agile organizational structure, efficient meeting formats, increased autonomy to teams and individuals, and a unique decision-making process.

The most defining principles of Holacracy include:

- Individuals hold multiple roles within the organization rather than a single job.
- Roles are grouped together in circles, with circles being connected through assigned roles called "lead links" and "rep links" which cannot be held by the same person.
- Roles and policies for the organization are created and updated using a clearly defined governance process.

- Orchestration of day-to-day operations and the managing of issues, known as tensions in the Holacracy world, rely on regular meetings, called "tactical meetings."
- The role of the traditional leader is subdivided and assigned to the most appropriate individual(s).
- Role assignments and circle structures can be changed at any time through the governance process.

The greatest benefits of Holacracy are role and process clarity. When executed well, there is little ambiguity in how things are to run and how decisions are to be made. It is an efficient system. Some argue that the efficiency of Holacracy comes at the expense of the human element. Others disagree.

There is a raging debate as to whether Holacracy is scalable beyond small teams. Zappos, once a scrappy scale-up and now an Amazon subsidiary, has developed a reputation for testing out radical ideas. In March of 2015, the company's CEO Tony Hsieh, announced the company was shifting to Holacracy.[1] Over two years later, the 1,500-employee company has become an ongoing case study on the pros and cons of this new way of working.

HolacracyOne provides a software platform called GlassFrog to administer the unique structures and meetings associated with Holacracy. Certified Holacracy consultants are available to assist with implementations and ongoing coaching.

Resourceful Humans and The RH-Way

The RH-Way started taking shape in 2009 while Heiko Fischer was the Global Head of Human Resources at video game maker, Crytek. An out-of-the-box thinker, Heiko's team began building a new approach to agile organizing suited to highly complex and dynamic industries like gaming. Heiko's work was heavily influenced by how Hewlett-Packard operated under its founders' tenure. Both Heiko and his father had been human resources leaders at HP when the company still lived by a philosophy known as "The HP Way."

With the tag line "100% Entrepreneurship, 0% Bureaucracy," the RH-Way turns purposeful organizations into entrepreneurial networks. Unlike traditional systems that put customers outside a company's organization, Resourceful Humans places the customer directly at the center of their management approach.

Resourceful Humans operates based on the following principles:

1. Give good people choices, including the ability to opt in or out of work contributions, and responsibility flourishes.
2. Create transparency of process, progress and results, and accountability ensues.
3. Keep it simple with responsibility for decision-making being nearest the customer, and collaboration thrives.

The RH-Way and supporting tools allow an organization to move from manager-led teams to a scaled network of self-governed teams. At the core is a leadership shift from an "approval" culture to a "veto" culture, and from long-term, top-line budgets to real time, bottom-line budgeting. By providing clarity of priority, the RH-Way empowers those closest to the customer to act autonomously. It is flexible in that it can be overlaid onto a traditional hierarchy or become a company's sole operating system.

Resourceful Humans is less refined in its marketing, global network and training resources for scale-ups than HolacracyOne. That said, the RH-Way appears to be more progressive on the technology front with the recent addition of virtual reality situational-leadership training. A number of large, multi-national companies are embracing the RH-Way and many smaller companies also rely on the approach for running their businesses.

The RH-Way is supported by three pieces of technology:

- netwoRHk is the primary tool used for mapping people's contributions in a visual network and tracking work progress across the organization in real time.
- staRHs is used to provide recognition and feedback with a virtual currency.
- caRHds supports running effective meetings.

Each tool can be used on its own or in conjunction with each other, bundled in the aiRH platform. Resourceful Humans also provides training and consulting support.

Teal Orgs from *Reinventing Organizations*

Frederic Laloux had been a longtime McKinsey consultant when he started noticing companies organizing in non-traditional ways. He took a deep interest in the subject and eventually left McKinsey to research these organizations full-time. His exploration led to the writing of *Reinventing Organizations*. The book has been defined by many as a game changer in the advancement of an ecosystemic approach to business.

Frederic's work is based on previous research around the levels of human consciousness. Each level of human consciousness has been assigned a color. The beliefs and characteristics associated with the "teal" consciousness level map with the organizations he describes.

Frederic's writing is centered on three breakthroughs: Self-management, Wholeness and Evolutionary Purpose. Rather than being presented as a defined system, Teal is a philosophy and way of being as an organization. Much like this book, he takes a look at many of the approaches used in traditional business and shares examples of alternatives more aligned with the Teal philosophy.

In addition to his books, Frederic and a network of his colleagues share the content of *Reinventing Organizations* broadly under a Creative Commons license, meaning anyone can use his work providing credit is given to the source. A helpful resource is the Reinventing Organizations Wiki.[2] There are a variety of consultants around the world who offer help to companies transitioning to Teal ways of working.

S3

The concept of sociocracy has its earliest roots in the 19th century. The term was originally coined to represent the science that studies how people organize themselves into social systems. Since then, it has gone through multiple iterations.

S3 is a framework based on sociocratic, holacratic, agile and lean methodologies. According to their website, S3 was "first conceived by Bernhard Bockelbrink and James Priest in 2014 and launched as an open source framework in March 2015."[3]

Much like Frederic's work in *Reinventing Organizations*, S3 centers on a set of basic principles.

- **Effectiveness** – Devote time only to what brings you closer to achieving your objectives.
- **Consent** – Do things in the absence of reasons not to.
- **Empiricism** – Test all assumptions through experiments, continuous revision and falsification.
- **Continuous Improvement** – Change incrementally to accommodate steady, empirical learning.
- **Equivalence** – People affected by decisions influence and change them on the basis of reasons to do so.
- **Transparency** – All information is available to everyone in an organization, unless there is a reason for confidentiality.

- **Accountability** – Respond when something is needed, do what you agreed to and take ownership for the course of the organization.

The concepts of S3 are shared through open distribution and a Creative Commons Free Culture license allowing anyone to use and apply the philosophies. The S3 team is available for consulting, learning facilitation, coaching and mentoring.

Finding Your Own Way

Different organizations have adopted the aforementioned methodologies in different ways. Fitzii, for example, follows the work of Frederic Laloux and *Reinventing Organizations* quite closely. Others have embraced Holacracy. Most, though, follow the path of Kurtis McBride at Miovision. Kurtis read about and researched many different philosophies and then customized an approach for his company.

Our intention is not to advocate for one approach over another but rather to invite exploration beyond traditional hierarchy.

Whatever path you choose to follow, we offer one piece of advice: when shifting to any new system or approach outside of a traditional hierarchy, recognize that it will be a journey. There is no guaranteed path to success. You can limit the challenges by learning from others, investing in training and coaching, and celebrating progress. Enjoy the journey; it is a gift in and of itself.

CONCLUDING...
FOR NOW

The epilogue to this book is yours alone. We hope you've discovered new and inspiring ideas and have expanded your thinking. We have not given you a standard framework or step-by-step guide. Instead, the resources here are offered as an invitation to iterate, experiment and evolve to suit your unique purpose.

Now it's time to get to work.

This guide is in perpetual beta, and we believe your company is too. The richness of *Reinventing Scale-Ups*, and its usefulness to you and others, will be made increasingly valuable through your contributions. Please let us know what experiments you run, what you learn, what succeeds, what fails and which practices change the game for you. Your willingness to create a different kind of world by creating a different kind of organization is significant. The world needs your courage, and moreover needs to hear your story—it is incumbent upon trailblazers to share success and failures. Doing so gives others confidence, which is needed now more than ever.

"... there is something about building up a comradeship—that I still believe is the greatest of all feats—and sharing in the dangers with your company of peers..."

– Sir Edmund Hillary

If you need help, reach out to us. **We're continuing the conversation on Facebook at https://www.facebook.com/ groups/ReinventingScaleUps** and would love to hear your story.

COMPANY PROFILES

While writing *Reinventing Scale-Ups*, some of our best learning came from exploring the new philosophies and practices emerging from the companies we interviewed. These organizations represent a tiny minority of all companies—the early adopters. They are blazing trails many others will follow.

These companies are inventing solutions to their unique challenges as they arise. There is great value in their ideas and experience. In the following pages we provide a deeper look inside six organizations and share their most unique attributes.

ECOSIA

The Company

Ecosia is a social business internet search engine. The company's differentiating factor is in how it uses funds raised from advertising revenues. Since it's founding, Ecosia has invested over €5M of profits planting 15 million trees. The Ecosia team has an audacious goal of planting 1 billion trees by 2020, a plan they admit will be difficult but achievable.

Company Stats

- Number of employees: 24 and growing
- Annual revenues: €10M
- Office location: Berlin (Germany)
- Interesting business fact: 175 million web searches monthly with 80% of profits going to support tree planting programs

CEO

While Christian Kroll was completing university studies in business administration, he was disappointed to learn most people saw profit-making as the only valid objective for a business. As his schooling came to an end, he decided he wanted to do something more meaningful with his energy and embarked on a year-long trip exploring the world. During his travels he learned about the important role of trees in our planet's survival. He returned from his adventure and started Ecosia in December 2009.

Culture Highlights

Purpose drives Ecosia's work. When team members get up Monday morning, they are drawn into work knowing their impact goes beyond computer code. It's a cause that team members can rally around and care about. This becomes even more poignant with monthly meetings including updates from the planting projects Ecosia is supporting.

Transparency is a second defining feature of Ecosia's culture. The company releases monthly financial reports online[1] providing a breakdown of how much money is going to salaries, user acquisition, tree planting and reserves.[1] They also publish a list of projects being funded.

Unique Elements

Values, Not Purpose, Get Used Every Day

When talking with the Ecosia team, it was core values that were continually referenced, not purpose.[2] They use the values lense for making all sorts of decisions. Should we scale? Should we work on improving the product? Are people pushing themselves too hard and becoming burnt out? Are we giving people good feedback? Ecosia's values include #Impact, #Integrity, #Sustainability, #Leadership, #User Focus and #Happiness. These words are hashtagged in internal communications when team members propose projects or changes that are values aligned. Each value is further defined using a short statement and brief paragraph.

Intentional Values Conflict

Should the team focus on improving the product or maximize profits for tree planting? The #User focus value encourages the former and #Impact suggests the latter. These are the hard yet necessary decisions required to keep Ecosia on track. Having conflicting values challenges the Ecosia team to consider trade-offs and find balance.

Values Retrospectives

With values being key to how Ecosia makes decisions, the team pauses from time-to-time to look at how their values are being used and asks, "Are these values still serving us well?" This process happens roughly every two years when someone feels called to bring it up. Ecosia does a great job examining, "What values are we exhibiting right now?" and "How do we know we are exhibiting those values?"

The Challenges of Being Purpose-based

There are two clear purpose-related challenges on the minds of people at Ecosia. The first is the ease with which individuals can become burnt out by getting too involved in their pursuit of purpose. As a first line of defense, the team names this as a possible issue so they collectively watch for it. Even still, they are continually aware of the hidden shadow of being a purpose-driven business and the stress it can place on the team.

The second challenge is trickier. The company's product funds, but is not directly tied to, its overarching purpose. Ecosia is built on top of Microsoft's Bing search engine infrastructure, meaning Ecosia has less control of its fate and ability to deliver on its purpose. The team is actively aware that fulfilling its purpose may require dramatic change in the future. Balancing short-term and long-term purpose is a tension within Ecosia's business. They've made a decision to stay the course for the time being.

To learn more about Ecosia, visit their website at www.ecosia. org.

Company Profile

ENSPIRAL

The Company

Enspiral is a collective of 150 entrepreneurs, changemakers and activists from around the world. They come together to work on systemic challenges and to support one another to do the work that matters to each individual contributor. Unlike a traditional company, Enspiral is a community of relationships rather than an employer. Members and contributors can form companies, act as freelancers or earn their livelihood in more traditional organizations. Enspiral is the place from which they support and amplify each other's purpose and build their livelihood.

Since 2010, Enspiral has been prototyping and growing; in the process, proving individuals can choose to band together and break free from a traditional economic system which funnels talents into formal organizations and bureaucracies. Instead, Enspiral is anchored in purpose, meaning and service.

Enspiral is at the forefront of the global self-organizing movement, exploring how cooperatives of entrepreneurs can support each other without being beholden to traditional investment and equity-based funding.

Company Stats

- Locations: Contributors in 20+ countries with founding roots in Wellington (New Zealand)
- Stewardship: 26 Members holding one nonfinancial share each
- Contributors: 150+
- Interesting business fact: Enspiral Ventures (companies born of Enspiral) include Loomio, Greaterthan, Enspiral Dev Academy, Fairground, EXP and many more.
- Interesting culture fact: Contributors participate in both the governance and collective budgeting of Enspiral and in working groups, are active in online communications and come together for bi-annual retreats.

Leadership

Enspiral is a bossless organization where anyone can self-select in to or out of working group participation. Every person and company associated with the Enspiral network is self-governing, with little guidance from the wider network. Enspiral is governed by open, transparent agreements. Legal compliance is held by a Minimum Viable Board (MVB) of Enspiral Foundation Limited, the central company-node of the community.

Individuals known as "Catalysts" act as scanners who maintain an online improvements board and initiate working groups. These working groups are sometimes specific to a particular project such as organizing the annual Enspiral Summerfest, but can also be associated with ongoing workstreams (e.g. Stewardship).

Culture Highlights

Everything Enspiral does is transparent and available to the public, making it easy to get a taste of the network's culture. The *Enspiral Handbook*[1], *Enspiral Tales*[2] online magazine and Enspiral Improvements Board[3] each offer a lens into the network's philosophies and functioning.

Making sense of a dynamic swarm of more than 150 people requires a few signposts and maps. The *Enspiral Handbook* holds all the formal rules and informal guidelines that keep this community functioning with minimum friction. It's a public resource, free for anyone to read, learn from and copy, inspiring tens of thousands of readers every year.

Enspiral Tales is an online magazine written by dozens of people, collaboratively edited and funded by community members. It is a place to hear some of the many voices of Enspiral. The content ranges from forward-thinking pieces on the future of work and meditations on the nature of human relationships, to practical tips and tutorials for decentralized organizations.

Whenever someone has an idea for how the Enspiral network could be improved, it gets logged in the public Enspiral Improvements Board. This is the project management hub for all "network maintenance and upgrade" work: the engine room for this self-improving organization.

Unique Elements

Livelihood Pods

Livelihood Pods are a recent experiment in supporting people to secure livelihoods outside of a traditional employment contract.

People who wish to work together form micro-cooperatives (Livelihood Pods) with a capped size of six to eight people. These pods become the legal vehicle for individuals to engage in contracts, as well as providing a more supportive environment than is available to most solo freelancers. This allows for a diversity of approaches and lowers administrative costs in comparison to a single, large freelancer collective.

Retreats

Retreats have been key to growing the culture of the Enspiral network. Organized gatherings every six months act as the cultural heartbeat for the community. They provide a vital space for connection, sense-making, trust-building, shared commitment-making, collaboration, growth and fun!

Decision-Making

Loomio is a software tool for small scale digital democracy. It offers a shining example of how companies can be run without coercive hierarchy or extractive relationships. Loomio is an Enspiral Venture born when activists from the Occupy Movement met the social entrepreneurs at Enspiral. In addition to serving a broad and ever increasing customer base, Loomio is the primary decision-making platform used across the Enspiral network.

Budgeting

CoBudget is a tool for making collaborative financial decisions.[4] It acts a lot like an internal crowdfunding system where anyone can propose a project and people allocate funds to the projects they would like to see happen. Anyone in the Enspiral community can raise a "bucket" to request funding for a project—contributors decide which projects to support by contributing individual funds.

FITZII

The Company

Like so many companies, Fitzii is an overnight success many years in the making. Founded in 2011, Fitzii has grown from software startup to an all-in-one hiring solution. They help small to medium-sized businesses hire better, faster and more affordably. The team has worked hard to differentiate themselves in a crowded marketplace. They combine expert hiring services and tools with smart recruitment software, like the Fitzii Assessment which replaces resume screening with a predictive and time-saving evaluation.

Company Stats

- Number of customers: 500 – 1,000
- Annual revenues: $1M – $2M
- Number of employees: 15 and growing

- Office locations: Oakville and Toronto (Canada)
- Interesting business fact: Fitzii's software was originally designed to remove bias from employment screening
- Interesting culture fact: Fitzii has a perfect (100%) employee satisfaction score

Leadership

Fitzii is a self-managed organization with no single leader. Instead, leadership is dispersed across the team. The company is a wholly-owned subsidiary of the Ian Martin Group (IMG), which is a certified B Corp[1] with 167 employees across Canada, the United States and India. IMG is a third generation family-owned company now led by Tim Masson, the grandson of the original founder. Tim holds the title of Chief Steward, a role he takes seriously. Since succeeding his father in 2011, Tim has focused on evolving IMG into "North America's most progressive recruitment and project-staffing firm." As Chief Steward, Tim retains overall responsibility for stewarding Fitzii (which IMG purchased in 2014). In practice, he fully embraces Fitzii's self-management approaches and is systematically introducing many of Fitzii's practices into the larger IMG organization.

As a B Corp, IMG meets comprehensive standards measuring the company's impact on employees, suppliers, its community and the environment. The company's guiding purpose is to "connect people with meaningful work."

Culture Highlights

On Valentine's Day of 2015, Fitzii officially eliminated management functions and became a self-managing company. In doing so, they relied heavily on the principles outlined in Frederic Laloux's book *Reinventing Organizations*. The team has fully integrated self-management into their day-to-day operations.

Teammates at Fitzii genuinely care for each other and are drawn together through a common connection to the company's purpose. The Fitzii team has created an environment that encourages psychological safety and invites everyone to bring their whole selves to work.

The Fitzii culture operates on a foundation of "Radical Responsibility." There is an expectation that every team member will take full responsibility for maximizing their own impact and engagement. If a problem or opportunity arises, the first team member to notice it is responsible for owning the issue until it is solved or transitioned to an appropriate member of the team.

Unique Elements

Three-circle Structure

Fitzii is structured as three overlapping circles in a venn diagram: Growth, Product and Development (P&D), and Customer Hiring Success (HS). Where two circles meet, there is a defining question the two groups work to solve:

- Between Growth and HS: How can we get more customers using more services to their benefit?
- Between HS and P&D: How can we systemize an awesome customer experience that leads to higher average spend?
- Between P&D and Growth: How can we prioritize and develop features quickly to attract new customer groups while keeping Fitzii's software robust, secure and easy to use?

In the center, where all three circles overlap, is the "Strategy Cabal." Members of the Strategy Cabal come from the original three groups (Growth, P&D, HS). This center group has three distinct responsibilities:

- Facilitate the annual company strategy, planning and thematic goal-setting process.
- Prioritize and manage major projects to meet strategic goals (although projects can be proposed and led by anyone).
- Sense where or how the strategy is shifting and introduce major discussion points with the entire team.

Also in the center of the venn diagram are the practices which affect all Fitzii team members, including hiring, compensation, feedback, team building, monthly meetings and internal communications. Over time, Fitzii has developed unique practices in each of these areas. If any person would like to suggest a new practice or change, they propose the topic in a monthly team meeting "lightning round." If there's energy for the topic and it's "ripe," the team will either use Generative Decision-Making (see Chapter 7) to co-create a proposal, or people will be assigned to oversee further advice processing.

Rituals and Symbols

The Fitzii team believes rituals, symbols and routines are a critical component in maintaining their unique cultural attributes. To see symbols in action, visit the About Fitzii page on the company's website where you will find a symbolic representation of what's important to each member of the team.[2] Without reading a word, you will already have some insight into each individual.

To close out an individual's onboarding, the team has a ritual of asking the new joiner to share why they want to be part of the team, what they are leaving behind from their past and how they want to grow and be in the new team.

Feedback

Realizing feedback was an area needing improvement, the team decided to figure out how it could be instilled as a habit. After reviewing *The Power of Habit* by Charles Duhigg, they settled on the Trigger, Action, Reward model to shape a new practice. Fitzii's commitment to Radical Responsibility is the trigger for feedback. If an individual has an idea or piece of feedback that could help someone else on the team, Radical Responsibility dictates that the individual needs to act on it. The entire team is trained in providing feedback through a three-step process:

- Outline the **situation**.
- Describe the **behavior.**
- Share the **impact** it has had on the individual delivering the feedback.

Any feedback is received as a gift and comes with an expectation. The receiver is expected to respond through a second three-step process:

- Provide **thanks** for the courage and care needed in providing helpful feedback.
- **Inquire** further to ensure a full understanding of the feedback.
- **Repeat** back what you've heard.

By the end of the week in which the feedback is provided, the recipient is expected to show recognition of the feedback giver on the company's online message board, Yammer. Sharing the content of the feedback is optional. At the end of each month, the number of recognitions received for giving feedback are counted and the person who delivered the most feedback that month receives a fun prize.

Immediately after implementing this new process, the amount of feedback went way up, with the average person providing between five and ten pieces of feedback per month. As a follow along effect, the quality and depth of relationships and trust increased. The process of having difficult conversations brought people together.

To learn more about how Fitzii operates, check out: https://blog.fitzii.com/category/self-management-teal-practices/.

Company Profile

MENLO INNOVATIONS

The Company

Menlo Innovations is a software design and development company focused on applying agile practices. Menlo is founded on the idea that pair programming creates substantially better software and reduces the total cost of development and maintenance. Through the use of their software development practices, their software is more affordable over the long term because of dramatically increased supportability, lower bug rates and a host of other factors.

Company Stats

- Founded: 2001
- Annual revenues: $6-7M

- Number of employees: 42 and growing
- Office location: Ann Arbor, Michigan (United States)
- Interesting business fact: 3,000 to 4,000 people a year travel from all over the world to visit Menlo, study them and learn from them. Menlo completes one to three tours or classes per day.
- Interesting culture fact: Code is only written when two people are working together sharing one computer, no exceptions.

CEO

Prior to starting Menlo Innovations, Rich Sheridan was the VP of Product Development at a successful software company in Ann Arbor, Michigan. Rich realized he was no longer learning or experiencing joy in his work and set out to rediscover his passion for software development. Along the way he was exposed to an agile development approach based on working in pairs. Through much effort on his part, Rich was able to integrate pair programming into the software company where he worked. Unfortunately, that company was acquired and promptly shut down in 2001 amidst the biggest tech crash the world had ever seen. Unphased, Rich was so confident in this new approach to software development that he co-founded Menlo Innovations with James Goebel as COO.

Culture Highlights

Working in pairs is a cornerstone of Menlo's culture. There is a firm rule that developers cannot write code unless pairing with someone. In addition, Menlo also pairs non-developer jobs. This has included Project Managers, Quality Assurance and High-Tech Anthropologists®, Menlo's answer to UX designers. Paired work has provided Menlo with a tremendous advantage. They are able to scale up and scale down the number of people working on a project quickly, avoiding reliance on individual "rock star" coders for successful development. Most important is the volume of learning everyone experiences as part of their daily work.

For most software development companies, scaling up a project is tricky due to the time needed to train new team members on the existing code base. At Menlo, individuals work in pairs on a project for a week. After the week is over, the pair splits up and one or two new people join, making it possible to successfully double the number of developers on a project quickly. The even bigger boon comes when it's time to scale down. Instead of needing to keep multiple experts on a project, Menlo only requires one pair of programmers from the large pool who have previously worked on the project. There are no specialties of programming at Menlo, so everyone is capable of handling the entire project, from architecture to execution.

Unique Elements

Team-driven Hiring, Promoting and Firing (When Absolutely Necessary)

With so much of the work at Menlo being done in groups, the team has a big say in who they work with. When it comes to hiring, the two founders offer their input, but their voices are equal to everyone else's. The final hiring decision is owned completely by the team with the founders having no vote or veto.

Promotions are decided by the team as well. When someone has demonstrated increased skills and capabilities, the team convenes, discusses, decides and lets the individual know they're ready for the next level. If an individual feels they're ready, they can also start the process. The end result will be a promotion or feedback on what's still needed to advance to the next level.

Once someone is hired, the team takes it as their collective responsibility to make sure that person has every opportunity to succeed. It's like everyone is managing everyone else on the team. If you don't work well with someone, you can ask not to be paired with that individual. If a critical mass of people ask not to be paired with the same individual, it becomes clear the person may not be a fit for Menlo. The team convenes to make a decision. As soon as a decision to let someone go is made, one of the senior people on the team lets the person know. They focus on doing it compassionately and helping those people find their next job where their skills can be better utilized. It's not uncommon for previous employees to have had such a good experience that they bring work back to Menlo from their future companies.

Menlo is a place where women seem to thrive. In an industry where the percentage of women is commonly in the single digits, Menlo boasts a female employee ratio of 40 percent. In addition, eight of eleven of Menlo's most senior and highest paid software team members are women.

Transparency

Transparency in Pay

With the team responsible for promoting colleagues, everyone's pay is transparent. There is a chart on the wall where everyone can see the pay for everyone else in the company.

At Menlo, there are four major compensation levels, each with three to five levels within for a total of 18 levels. It's a linear progression in pay with each level representing a salary increase of about $5,000 annually.

It doesn't matter if you're an engineer, Project Manager or High-Tech Anthropologist®, everyone at Menlo is on the same pay scale. This encourages people to try out different roles without worrying about compensation implications. It also creates a culture of appreciation for the expertise of people in different roles.

Transparency in Financials

Transparency is an area Menlo is constantly seeking to expand. In 2016, Menlo began experimenting with making the company financials visible to everyone. It's an ongoing experiment with a retrospective at the end of each quarterly iteration to learn what was and wasn't useful. Each iteration leads to changes in the metrics being reported. They are also tweaking the process with respect to who researches and reports on the numbers in order to spread out financial reporting control.

Building in Flexibility

Like many service-based businesses, the money coming in to Menlo fluctuates month-to-month. The team has created many clever ways to manage these fluctuations, including having some team members pre-agree to work flexible hours. These individuals receive full medical benefits, but the hours worked monthly fluctuate based on their availability and Menlo's need. It's normally a win-win relationship. Sometimes business dips lower than this buffer can account for, a situation that happened in early 2016. Unlike most businesses, Menlo didn't look toward layoffs. Instead, everyone on the team stepped up and shared the burden of reduced hours and reduced pay. The team self-organizes around those individuals less able to handle a temporary reduction in compensation.

If you liked learning about Menlo Innovations, you can read more in the book *Joy, Inc.*, written by co-founder and CEO, Richard Sheridan, or at http://menloinnovations.com/.

Company Profile

MIOVISION

The Company

Miovision was founded in 2005 by three engineering graduates from the University of Waterloo. The company works with traffic data collection firms, engineering firms and government agencies to collect, analyze and act on traffic data. The result of their work is better traffic flow, less congestion and positive environmental impacts from reduced idling.

Company Stats

- Number of customers: 650 across 50 countries
- Number of employees: 160 and growing
- Office locations: Kitchener (Canada), Cologne (Germany)
- Interesting business fact: 3.3+ billion vehicles counted
- Interesting culture fact: Near zero voluntary turnover

CEO

Miovision is led by CEO and co-founder Kurtis McBride. Early in Kurtis' leadership, he struggled with the same challenge faced by most founder CEOs: how does one lead others when accustomed to doing everything on their own? In Kurtis' words, "You know how to do things but not necessarily how to build teams that can do things." This is especially difficult when building a business where everyone is bright, talented and encouraged to contribute equally. Over time, Kurtis has applied his research, design and prototyping skills to creating an empowered environment that serves his business well.

Culture Highlights

Miovision's culture is a work-in-progress. Kurtis has a vision for how the organization can operate more effectively and works with the team to experiment. The cultural highlights and unique practices listed below are being tested and refined as part of Miovision's journey.

At the core of Miovision's culture are two philosophies—one applies to individual contributors and the other to business leaders. Kurtis refers to these as "first principles."

For individual contributors, Miovision believes that the ideal role for every team member exists at the intersection of **passion, skill and need**. Passion is uniquely personal to each individual. The skill match is negotiated between the company and the team member. Need is articulated through defined business goals. Miovision is relentless in making sure passion, skill and need overlap for everyone on the team.

Miovision has managers and leaders, but not in the traditional sense. Through prototyping, Kurtis came to realize there are three distinct components to management—strategy, execution and empathy, with empathy defined as knowing how to work with people to get the best performance. Strategy, execution and empathy are distinct in the skills, aptitudes and experiences required for success. Asking one person to excel in all three is unrealistic, yet most companies have this expectation. Not at Miovision. Over time, managers are identified as having a superpower in one of these three areas. As a result, certain individuals must be involved in making strategic decisions, others in day-to-day execution and others in enhancing human performance. The people filling these roles are referred to as "lead nodes." Each lead node is empowered to make decisions within a defined scope aligned with their superpower.

What happens if two lead nodes disagree? At different times, different lead nodes are prioritized. One year, culture might be a higher priority and therefore the empathy leads would be the tiebreakers. At other times, execution might be the priority and those leads would break the tie. As much as possible, teams are encouraged to solve issues without needing a tiebreaker. At Miovision, the result is less bureaucracy and better outcomes.

Since implementing this model, Miovision's employee Net Promoter Score[1] (eNPS) has jumped by more than 25 percent.

Unique Elements

The 3-Decision Rule

In a truly empowered environment, differences in opinion can result in deadlocks. Enter the 3-Decision Rule. As its name suggests, this tactic allows each leader to break with empowerment and unblock deadlocks up to three times a year. Because the power to break deadlocks is a scarce commodity, it is reserved for the most critical situations. Most decisions are sent back to the team to continue looking for common ground.

Tribal Accountability

Miovision uses "tribal accountability" rather than leader-driven, top-down tactics. The company relies on the sense of responsibility inherent in daily stand-up meetings, open team presentations of progress and weekly/monthly company meeting formats. In Kurtis' words, "These meetings create public discussion and commitments, break down silos and distribute accountability through the team."

Mobility Constrained Only by Need

Miovision aims to have every team member working at the intersection of passion, skill and need. Since all three parameters evolve over time, Miovision limits internal movement only by need. If a team member's passions change or skills grow, they are free to seek out a new role anywhere in the company. The only requirement is that the new role serves a company need. This freedom of mobility allows team members to reinvent their career within Miovision over and over again.

Leadership Tables Are Open

Based on the first principle of separating strategy, execution and empathy between individuals, Miovision does not have a single defined leadership team. Attendance at the company's weekly leadership team meeting is based on that week's agenda. All leadership meetings are open to everyone in the company. Anyone who chooses to attend is expected to contribute in areas where they have expertise. Does this lead to a room overflowing with participants? In reality, the same small group of people gather each week with occasional additions.

To learn more about how Miovision works, check out: https://miovision.com/blog/top-10-tactics-for-managing-in-an-empowered-environment/.

Company Profile

PERCOLAB

The Company

Percolab's consulting, training and facilitation services help
create the conditions for great collaboration. Companies,
governments and NGOs hire Percolab to grow future-
oriented ways of working and learning with more humanness.
Organizational transformation may take the form of large
scale structural change or the introduction of small practices
that grow new mindsets. Percolab is engaged in both realms.
The company works with complexity, collective intelligence,
collaborative practices, collective sense-making and visual
thinking.

Company Stats

- Year founded: 2007
- Number of employees / contributors: 25 and growing

- Size of client organizations: 2 to 150,000 employees
- Office locations: Montreal (Canada), Montpellier (France), Brussels (Belgium) and Barcelona (Spain)
- Interesting culture fact: All team meetings are open to outside guests, with 2-3 guests typically joining each meeting

Leadership

Percolab is a self-governed international community with no single leader. Each local hub is an independent legal structure with its own self-managing system, and is in tune with its local context. All hubs share the same charter and connect to work related to a human-centered future. Leadership is distributed into explicit organizational roles, both at the local level and the international level. These roles rotate amongst community members and employees. Percolab is a balance between distributed authority and collective decision-making using a Generative Decision-Making process.

Culture Highlights

As a project-based company, Percolab welcomes professionals who want the autonomy of freelancing and seek the benefits of being part of a team. The organization is pioneering its own innovative organizational model based on ecosystemic thinking.

Since it's founding, Percolab has offered massive flexibility and autonomy to employees and contributors, and been highly participatory in the way it functions. In 2015, the organization went a step further and brought in a formal self-managing system with explicit roles. They have also shifted to a conscious compensation model (outlined below).

All Percolab employees work in client projects and co-manage all aspects of the company with the support of external expertise.

Each individual is accountable for a few management roles that can shift or evolve anytime at anyone's request. There is a collective role check-in every three months. The priority of those meetings is to keep roles current and ensure individuals make good use of their expertise while feeling challenged in their own personal growth.

Employees are expected to attend 70 percent of weekly team meetings, either in-person or virtually, and to come into the office at least two days a week. Hence, there is an extreme amount of leeway in where and when a person works. This allows employees to create the lifestyle they want while also caring for the work, their clients and the team. The result? Percolab members travel extensively, write books, invest in educational projects and are dedicated parents and grandparents.

Unique Elements

Conscious Compensation Model

For Percolab, it is important that individuals have agency over how much they work and earn. Money is not a taboo topic but a conscious practice. The company functions with "variable self-set salaries." This means that each individual negotiates the portion of a project budget that goes to them based on the value of their contribution. Each month, an individual can be involved in multiple projects, therefore the sum of the financial agreements is their salary for the month. The project team needs to ensure a feeling of fairness in how the project budget is distributed. This can invite real conversations that help individuals be more realistic about the value of their contributions.

The Percolab compensation model is a blend of the stability and regularity of a traditional employment model, with the flexibility and autonomy of a freelancer model. With this system, work that is outside of projects, such as attending team meetings or networking, is not directly compensated. Percolab thinks it is healthy to have some "non-transactional" labor as a way to gather clarity around the team's relationship with money.

Company Retreats

Since relationships are central to the culture, annual three-day team retreats are a priority at Percolab. Members go into nature together and dig into deeper co-learning as well as cultural and strategic issues. It is a time to deepen the fellowship amongst members.

Not only do members co-organize and attend retreats with their local company, it is encouraged to attend retreats organized by Percolab companies in other jurisdictions. This is a way of growing a wider Percolab community that supports and learns from each other.

Radical Openness

The methods and practices Percolab develops are shared with the world for everyone's learning and use. All finances are open to the members, including salaries. Team meetings are open to outside guests who come to discover how an organization can run differently. Percolab team meetings integrate operational, governance and sense-making themes in a fluid manner. Together, the group naturally rotates meeting roles—framing, facilitation, documentation, timekeeping and energy monitoring.

Guests join these meetings for a variety of reasons—an interest in collaborating with Percolab; to study the organization; to learn about self-management; or simply for the opportunity of networking. Since collective decision-making is consent-based, it is also an open process in which everyone has a voice, including guests. The premise is that collective intelligence strengthens the decisions.

To learn more about how Percolab operates, check out: http://www.percolab.com/en/blog/.

THE AUTHORS

Brent Lowe

Brent is The Scale Coach for Founder CEOs. His firsthand experience comes from founding and growing four companies, as well as serving on the leadership teams of three successful founder-led companies. Brent helped those organizations double revenues, launch new businesses, integrate acquisitions and expand globally.

As a coach and author, Brent works with entrepreneurs and business leaders to conquer the steep learning curve that comes with rapid growth. Many of his clients are focused on solving problems related to the UN's Sustainable Development Goals.

Brent holds a Bachelor in Engineering and Management, an MBA, an MA in Counseling Psychology and a certificate in Small and Medium-Sized Enterprise Board Effectiveness. He lives in Toronto, Canada.

Susan Basterfield

Having lived and worked in 20 different countries, Susan chose New Zealand as home in 2003.

Proof that 25 years working in multi-nationals is a reversible condition, today Susan serves the Enspiral Foundation as a Director and Catalyst, and does her work from within an Enspiral Livelihood Pod.

As a catalyst and convener, she helps individuals and organizations release potential through participatory creation—unique manifestations of ways of working and being beyond traditional hierarchical models. These include ongoing experiments in Self-Management, Agile Beyond Tech, Deliberately Developmental Organizations, and Facilitative Leadership. She is a prolific writer and speaker, and has shared her experiences from India to Korea, Canada to Chile, Sweden to Australia and most places in between.

Her broader focus is on building digital learning platforms and communities of purpose and intentional practice, testing her hypothesis that our transition into what's next will be brought about by and through community. Susan is the creator and convener of the Practical Self Management Intensive at Leadwise Academy. She holds a BA in Communications, a Postgraduate Diploma in Teaching and Learning, and in 2015, received the Perkins Award for most exceptional body of work in the second cohort of Seth Godin's altMBA.

Travis Marsh

Travis is the founder of Tap In, a software company bringing executive coaching to the mainstream. He started the company as a way to scale the impact that's possible when people become clear on what and how they want to develop, and are willing to take action to make it happen. This company grew out of Travis' other work as a facilitator and coach.

Travis facilitates Interpersonal Communication classes at the Stanford Graduate School of Business. He coaches early to mid-stage startups and entrepreneurs. His clients work at companies including Facebook, Google, Amazon, Netflix, Microsoft, AirBnB, Uber and Stripe, but he specializes in assisting fast growth, VC-funded companies.

The thread connecting these endeavours is a desire to unleash people's potential by aligning individuals with their intrinsic motivations. His experience stems from growing successful sales teams at startups in Silicon Valley. Travis graduated as Salutatorian from the University of Florida College of Engineering and is an International Coach Federation Certified Coach.

Travis lives and works in San Francisco, California.

REFERENCES

Introduction
1. http://www.reinventingorganizations.com/
2. http://a.co/9c3fbJ1
3. http://brenebrown.com/books-audio/
4. https://www.ted.com/talks/brene_brown_on_vulnerability

Chapter 1 – Why This Book? Why Now?
1. http://agilemanifesto.org/

Chapter 2 – Looking Inward First
1. https://www.greenleaf.org/what-is-servant-leadership/

Chapter 3 – Bringing Meaning to Work
1. http://www.jonhaworth.com/toys/mission-statement-generator
2. http://bit.ly/WhanganuiRiver
3. http://bit.ly/RSU-Link32

4. http://bit.ly/RSU-Link33
5. https://unreasonable.is/mission-vision-values-forget-it/
6. https://www.southwest.com/html/about-southwest/
7. http://dna.crisp.se/
8. http://bit.ly/LeipzigTedTalk
9. https://hbr.org/2016/03/4-hard-questions-to-ask-about-your-companys-purpose

Chapter 4 – Creating the Strongest Teams

1. http://bit.ly/Google-PS-Study

Chapter 5 – Adult-to-Adult Relationships

2. http://bit.ly/DK-Commitments
1. https://hbr.org/2012/04/to-ensure-great-teamwork-start
2. http://www.valvesoftware.com/company/Valve_Handbook_LowRes.pdf
3. https://handbook.enspiral.com/
4. http://www.self-managementinstitute.org/path/CLOU

Chapter 6 – Matching Strengths to Needs

1. https://www.amazon.com/dp/B00S590OQI
2. http://www.percolab.com/en/self-management-roles-and-process-design

Chapter 7 – How to Decide

1. http://a.co/1rYxc2N
2. https://www.loomio.org/
3. https://app.cloverpop.com/
4. Adapted from "Holacracy's Integrative Decision Making Process" by Itamar Goldminz – http://bit.ly/RSU-Link71
5. http://www.artofhosting.org/
6. http://bit.ly/RSU-Link72

7. https://handbook.enspiral.com/agreements/decisions.html

Chapter 8 – Working Without Blinders
1. https://en.wikipedia.org/wiki/Kanban_board
2. https://en.wikipedia.org/wiki/Sprint_(software_development)
3. https://en.wikipedia.org/wiki/Burn_down_chart

Chapter 9 – Being Deliberately Developmental
1. https://www.radicalcandor.com/the-book/
2. https://www.cnvc.org/Training/NVC-Concepts
3. https://www.wibas.com/scrum/5-steps-of-a-retrospective/en
4. http://www.retrium.com/

Chapter 10 – Sustaining What Matters
1. https://open.buffer.com/27-question-to-ask-instead-of-what-do-you-do/
2. http://amandafenton.com/2014/04/check-in-question-ideas/

Chapter 11 – The Taboo Topic of Compensation
1. http://bit.ly/RSU-Link111
1. https://open.buffer.com/transparent-salaries/
2. http://bit.ly/EnspiralRS
3. http://bit.ly/EnspiralGP
4. http://bit.ly/HolacracyOneComp
5. http://slicingpie.com/
6. https://open.buffer.com/transparent-pricing-buffer/

Chapter 12 – Choosing Future Colleagues
1. http://bit.ly/DK-12Keys
2. http://wellbeingteams.org/

3. https://journal.leadwise.co/recruitment-as-dating-14383fd-e5dfe

Chapter 13 – The New Joiner Experience

1. http://bit.ly/RSU-Link131

Chapter 14 – Moving Beyond Traditional Hierarchies

1. https://www.fastcompany.com/3044417/zappos-ceo-tony-hsieh-adopt-holacracy-or-leave
2. www.reinventingorganizationswiki.com
3. http://sociocracy30.org/

Ecosia

1. http://ecosia.dropmark.com/369415?page=1
2. http://documents.ecosia.org/374680/8921345

Enspiral

1. http://handbook.enspiral.com
2. http://blog.enspiral.com
3. http://improvements.enspiral.com
4. www.cobudget.com

Fitzi

1. http://www.bcorporation.net/
2. https://www.fitzii.com/go/about/

Miovision

1. http://www.netpromotersystem.com/about/employee-engagement.aspx

70432917R00108